SpringerBriefs in Business

SpringerBriefs present concise summaries of cutting-edge research and practical applications across a wide spectrum of fields. Featuring compact volumes of 50 to 125 pages, the series covers a range of content from professional to academic. Typical topics might include:

- A timely report of state-of-the art analytical techniques
- A bridge between new research results, as published in journal articles, and a contextual literature review
- A snapshot of a hot or emerging topic
- An in-depth case study or clinical example
- A presentation of core concepts that students must understand in order to make independent contributions

SpringerBriefs in Business showcase emerging theory, empirical research, and practical application in management, finance, entrepreneurship, marketing, operations research, and related fields, from a global author community.

Briefs are characterized by fast, global electronic dissemination, standard publishing contracts, standardized manuscript preparation and formatting guidelines, and expedited production schedules.

Francesca Sanguineti

The Organizational Impact of Patient Engagement

Enhancing the Healthcare Journey

Springer

Francesca Sanguineti
Department of Economics and Management
University of Pavia
Pavia, Italy

ISSN 2191-5482 ISSN 2191-5490 (electronic)
SpringerBriefs in Business
ISBN 978-3-031-77963-3 ISBN 978-3-031-77964-0 (eBook)
https://doi.org/10.1007/978-3-031-77964-0

This Springer imprint is published by the registered company Springer Nature Switzerland AG
The registered company address is: Gewerbestrasse 11, 6330 Cham, Switzerland

Letter from the Vice President of Fondazione Mondino IRCCS

Dear Reader,

As the Vice President of Fondazione Mondino IRCCS and the Pro-Rector of the University of Pavia, I am pleased to introduce this contribution to the field of patient engagement and healthcare management. This work is the result of a collaboration between our institutions, highlighting the power of bridging academic research with practical insights.

Fondazione Mondino has at its core a strict collaboration with the academic world. Yet, the managerial and organizational outcomes of these collaborations are often underexplored. This book helps advance the field by investigating the practical implications of patient engagement strategies on the process efficiency of healthcare organizations.

I encourage you to delve into the insights and practical recommendations presented here, as they have the potential to drive improvements in healthcare delivery and patient outcomes. I believe this work will inspire further research and discussions on the importance of addressing patient journey touchpoints at both the organizational and departmental levels, ultimately leading to a positive impact on healthcare organizations as a whole.

Best regards,

Pietro Previtali
Vice President, Fondazione Mondino IRCCS
Pro-Rector, University of Pavia, Italy

Letter from the General Manager of Fondazione Mondino IRCCS

Dear Reader,

As the General Manager of Fondazione Mondino IRCCS, I witness firsthand the importance of placing patients at the center of their care journey. It is with great pleasure that I present to you this book, which offers an overview of patient engagement, drawing upon a systematic literature review and an in-depth case study of our institution.

This work shows part of our journey toward patient-centered care, and we look forward to seeing the positive results that will emerge from implementing the insights and recommendations here presented.

I believe that the insights presented will provide the basis for healthcare organizations as they strive to improve patient outcomes and organizational efficiency in an ever-evolving landscape.

I commend the author for her dedication to this important topic for both the patients and the organizations.

Sincerely,

Gianni Bonelli

General Manager, Fondazione Mondino IRCCS

Preface

Patients have increasingly been recognized as active actors in their own journeys, and patient engagement has emerged as a fundamental driver in improving health outcomes and enhancing the quality of care. As a researcher in organization studies, I have been attracted to the potential effects that patient engagement strategies have on organizational efficiency, as I believe these could provide the leverage healthcare organizations need to really start addressing this point effectively.

Therefore, this book represents the outcome of extensive research and collaborations, with the main aim of shedding light on the current state of patient engagement practices and their impact on healthcare organizations. With this work, I have sought to provide practical insights and recommendations for healthcare leaders, managers, and professionals.

Fondazione Mondino IRCCS, a center of excellence in the Pavia district known for its healthcare quality and its university, represents a significant case study, demonstrating the value of collaboration between academia and healthcare institutions. Thanks to this partnership, we have gained important insights into the strategies employed by the organization and the potential future steps.

The ideas and findings presented in this book are the result of the collective efforts of managers, researchers, management students, and healthcare professionals, whom I want to thank for their time, contributions, and expertise.

Besides the individuals directly involved in the data collection process, I want to thank Pietro, who convinced me to embark on this project and supported me along the way. Thank you for always pushing me beyond my comfort limits. I also want to extend my deepest gratitude to the people who have never stopped believing in me: Mum and Dad, I would not be where I am if it weren't for you. Uncle Paolo, thank you for listening to my venting and brainstorming with me. Last, but definitely not least, to my biggest supporters, Daniele and Federica, for their daily—often annoying—reminders.

Pavia, Italy | Francesca Sanguineti

Contents

Chapter 1
Introduction

Abstract As healthcare systems face rising costs, aging populations, and the growing prevalence of chronic diseases, one solution holds transformative potential: patient engagement. By empowering patients as active partners in their care, healthcare organizations can achieve better outcomes, improved quality, and enhanced efficiency (Coulter, 2017; Graffigna et al., 2014). This book explores the power of patient engagement through a systematic literature review and a case study of Fondazione Mondino IRCCS, a leading neurological hospital in Italy. Highlighting the critical yet often overlooked role of the front office, it introduces the Patient Engagement at Front Office (PEFO) framework. This practical tool emphasizes digital integration, staff empowerment, environment optimization, information clarity, and feedback loops. Providing actionable strategies, this book offers healthcare leaders insights to redefine patient experiences, driving meaningful improvements in care delivery and organizational performance.

As healthcare systems face exceptional challenges, from rising costs to aging populations and the growing issue of chronic diseases, the need for innovative solutions has never been more pressing (Anderson-Wallace & Downham, 2023). At the core of this needed transformation lies the concept of patient engagement—a shift in the way we think about and deliver healthcare services. By placing patients at the center of their own care, empowering them to take an active role in decision-making, and fostering meaningful partnerships between patients and providers, healthcare organizations have the potential to achieve better health outcomes, improve the quality of care, and enhance organizational efficiency (e.g., Coulter, 2017; Graffigna et al., 2014; Hibbard and Greene, 2013).

This book aims to offer an exploration of patient engagement strategies and their impact on healthcare organizations' efficiency, drawing upon a systematic review of the existing literature and an in-depth case study of Fondazione Mondino, a leading neurological hospital and research center in Italy. By synthesizing insights from these two approaches, we provide a better understanding of the current state of patient engagement research and practice, identify key challenges and

F. Sanguineti, *The Organizational Impact of Patient Engagement*,
SpringerBriefs in Business, https://doi.org/10.1007/978-3-031-77964-0_1

opportunities, and propose a novel framework for enhancing patient engagement at a fundamental touchpoint in the healthcare journey—the front office.

The concept of patient engagement reflects a shift from a provider-centric model of care to one that recognizes patients as active partners in their own health and well-being (Graffigna & Barello, 2018). Engaged patients are more likely to adhere to treatment plans, make informed decisions about their care, and experience better health outcomes (Krist et al., 2017). Moreover, patient engagement strategies have been shown to lead to improvements in healthcare quality, safety, and efficiency by incorporating patient perspectives and experiences into care delivery processes (Bombard et al., 2018).

Despite the growing evidence supporting the benefits of patient engagement, healthcare organizations often struggle to implement effective strategies, particularly in the early stages of the patient journey. The front office, as one of the initial points of contact between patients and the healthcare system, represents an important yet often overlooked opportunity to set the stage for a proper patient engagement. Indeed, by starting with this touchpoint, healthcare organizations can lay the foundation for patient engagement that extends throughout their entire journey.

The systematic literature review presented in Chap. 2 provides a comprehensive overview of the current state of research on patient engagement strategies and their impact on healthcare organizations' efficiency. By synthesizing findings from a diverse range of studies, we identify themes, gaps, and avenues for future research, highlighting the need for more targeted interventions in the early stages of the patient journey.

Chapter 3 delves into the organizational background and evolution of the Italian National Health Service, setting the context for the case study of Fondazione Mondino. Examining the challenges and opportunities faced by healthcare organizations operating within this system, we offer insights into the factors that might shape patient engagement efforts in a specific national context. We then present Fondazione Mondino in detail to properly introduce the case.

In Chap. 4, we explore patient engagement organizational strategies at Fondazione Mondino. We map the patient journey for three common neurological conditions—multiple sclerosis, Parkinson's disease, and headache disorders—to identify the most important touchpoints and the related rising opportunities for patient engagement. A particular focus is placed on the role of the front office in shaping patient experiences and perceptions, revealing both best practices and areas for improvement.

Drawing upon the insights derived from the systematic review and the case study, Chap. 5 proposes the Patient Engagement at Front Office (PEFO) framework. The novelty lies in proposing a structured approach aimed at enhancing patient engagement and organizational efficiency at the beginning of the patient journey. The framework consists of five core components: digital integration, staff empowerment, environment optimization, information clarity, and feedback loop. The PEFO framework offers healthcare organizations a practical tool for operationalizing patient-centered care principles and developing strategies for improvement.

This book represents a timely contribution to the field of patient engagement and healthcare management. We provide a comprehensive understanding of the current state of research and practice, identify key challenges and opportunities, and propose a novel framework for enhancing patient engagement at right from the front office operations. As healthcare organizations worldwide strive to adapt to the evolving needs and expectations of patients, the insights and recommendations presented in this book offer guidance for improvements in care delivery.

References

Anderson-Wallace, M., & Downham, N. (2023). *Improving quality in healthcare: Questioning the work for effective change*. Sage Publications.

Bombard, Y., Baker, G. R., Orlando, E., Fancott, C., Bhatia, P., Casalino, S., & Pomey, M. P. (2018). Engaging patients to improve quality of care: A systematic review. *Implementation Science, 13*, 1–22.

Coulter, A. (2017). Measuring what matters to patients. *BMJ, 356*, j816. https://doi.org/10.1136/bmj.j816. PMID: 28219884.

Graffigna, G., & Barello, S. (2018). Patient health engagement (PHE) model in enhanced recovery after surgery (ERAS): Monitoring patients' engagement and psychological resilience in minimally invasive thoracic surgery. *Journal of Thoracic Disease, 10*(Suppl 4), S517.

Graffigna, G., Barello, S., Riva, G., & Bosio, C. (2014). Patient engagement: The key to redesign the exchange between the demand and supply for healthcare in the era of active ageing. *Active Ageing and Healthy Living: A Human Centered Approach in Research and Innovation as Source of Quality of Life, 203*, 85.

Hibbard, J. H., & Greene, J. (2013). What the evidence shows about patient activation: Better health outcomes and care experiences; fewer data on costs. *Health Affairs, 32*(2), 207–214.

Krist, A. H., Tong, S. T., Aycock, R. A., & Longo, D. R. (2017). Engaging patients in decision-making and behavior change to promote prevention. *Information Services & Use, 37*(2), 105–122.

Chapter 2
A Systematic Review of Patient Engagement and Its Organizational Impact

Abstract Patient engagement has emerged as an important element in healthcare, shifting patients from passive recipients to active contributors in their care. While its benefits for health outcomes are well-documented, its impact on healthcare organizations' efficiency remains underexplored. This chapter presents a systematic review of the literature, synthesizing current research on patient engagement strategies and their organizational implications. By examining diverse approaches, such as digital tools, shared decision-making, and patient education, the review highlights gaps in understanding the broader impact of engagement on process efficiency. It also identifies key research streams, main theoretical perspectives, and practical strategies. The findings provide insights and a roadmap for future research to optimize patient engagement in healthcare organizations.

2.1 Introduction

In the contemporary healthcare domain, an involved patient represents more than just a recipient of care but rather a crucial partner in the pursuit of efficacy and productivity (Byrne et al., 2020). This represents the recent point of view which perceives patient engagement as an essential element of healthcare systems (Barello et al., 2012; Saut et al., 2023). Indeed, as healthcare organizations worldwide strive to enhance results and reduce inefficiencies, the role of the patient is increasingly that of an active contributor rather than that of a passive receiver (Alharbi et al., 2014; Van den Borne, 1998). Yet, most studies still underestimate the potential effects that enhancing patient engagement might have on the organization's process efficiency (Bertorello et al., 2022; Irizarry et al., 2015; Laurance et al., 2014). This first chapter of the book adopts a systematic literature review approach with the aim of examining the extent to which patient engagement strategies impact healthcare organizations.

Patient engagement works as a tactic that integrates the patient's perspective into the clinical process, with the aim of achieving superior health results and more streamlined healthcare procedures (Graffigna & Barello, 2018a, b; Ivany et al.,

F. Sanguineti, *The Organizational Impact of Patient Engagement*,
SpringerBriefs in Business, https://doi.org/10.1007/978-3-031-77964-0_2

2023). The underlying premise is that well-informed and engaged patients can help in the decision-making process, thus amplifying the suitability and efficiency of care (Krist et al., 2017). In fact, research increasingly found that patient-centered care models, which focus on patient engagement, are linked to reduced healthcare service usage, decreased costs, and improved patient results (Bertakis & Azari, 2011; Engle et al., 2021; Miller, 2016).

To establish a proper understanding of this dynamic, the study presented in this chapter describes the methodologies, scopes, and diverse strategies of patient engagement within the patient journey's steps. By employing a well-established methodology, the systematic literature review, we examine the extensive range of existing literature and report the main results. The methodological framework involved a detailed search of the four mostly used databases, including PubMed, Google Scholar, Scopus, and Web of Science (Hickmann et al., 2022; Jones et al., 2011). The inclusion and exclusion criteria were defined a priori, and two other researchers were asked to revise the manuscripts' selection. Articles not in English or those deviating from the research question were excluded from the analysis (please refer to Sect. 2.2 for further details).

By providing a clear picture of the current state of the art of patient engagement and its impact on healthcare organizations, stakeholders could better plan and implement interventions that are both effective and sustainable. The goal is to highlight the importance of fostering an environment where patient engagement is not an optional add-on but a fundamental aspect of healthcare delivery that contributes to the overall improvement of healthcare organizations and systems.

2.2 Context and Methodology

2.2.1 Context

Patient engagement is increasingly considered as a fundamental element of efficient healthcare provision, significantly impacting both outcomes and costs (Alkhatib et al., 2024; World Health Organization, 2016). Given the rise in costs, aging demographics, and the increasing incidence of chronic diseases challenging healthcare systems globally, the enhancement of patient engagement has emerged as a fundamental tactic (Alkhatib et al., 2024; Graffigna et al., 2014). The notion of patient engagement includes efforts directed at engaging patients in their own healthcare, including shared decision-making, self-management education, and the utilization of digital health tools (Barello et al., 2012; Schoenfeld et al., 2016).

The necessity to engage patients lies in its capacity to improve health results while reducing healthcare costs (Alkhatib et al., 2024; Krist et al., 2017). Engaged patients are more inclined to comply with treatment regimens, access preventive services, and avoid costly emergency interventions, thereby potentially improving the overall healthcare organizations' efficacy (Marzban et al., 2022). Moreover, patient engagement has been characterized as the "blockbuster drug of the century"

(Chase, 2012; Rieckmann et al., 2015, p. 204), underscoring its transformative influence on healthcare provision (Carman et al., 2013).

The significance of patient engagement is further underscored by its association with enhanced health outcomes, reduced costs, and heightened satisfaction with care (Marzban et al., 2022). For instance, enhancing patient health literacy is pivotal for effective engagement, as it facilitates informed decision-making and a deeper comprehension of health-related information (Daack-Hirsch & Campbell, 2014; Snow, 2022). A well-informed patient is more inclined to actively engage in their healthcare, leading to improved health behaviors and outcomes (Bombard et al., 2018; Graffigna & Barello, 2017).

Despite the acknowledged advantages, the impact of patient engagement on healthcare and, more specifically, on the healthcare organization's efficiency remains insufficiently explored (e.g., Alkhatib et al., 2024; Marzban et al., 2022; Merker et al., 2022). Current studies frequently concentrate on specific facets of engagement or particular diseases, creating a gap in understanding its broader implications (Alkhatib et al., 2024). Addressing this gap can be important for healthcare providers and policymakers willing to put into practice effective engagement strategies that can drive to improvement in healthcare organizations efficiency.

Moreover, the healthcare landscape is rapidly evolving with technological advancements, policy adaptations, and changes in patient expectations (e.g., Ćwiklicki et al., 2020). These dynamics highlight the necessity for a comprehensive investigation of how patient engagement approaches can be included in the provision of healthcare to improve organizations and their efficiency (Alkhatib et al., 2024; Engle et al., 2021; Li et al., 2023). This systematic literature review aims to comprehensively synthetize the current state of the art with a methodology that is proven to reduce biases as it follows strict protocols (Denyer & Tranfield, 2009; Tranfield et al., 2003).

By addressing the research question, "How do patient engagement strategies impact healthcare organizations' process efficiency?", this chapter aims to provide a detailed understanding of the mechanisms through which engagement may influence organizational efficiency. It also seeks to highlight the current state of the art on the topic and propose areas for future research to optimize patient engagement efforts in healthcare organizations. The outcome of our study provides guidance for future research, as the identified gaps are crucial for academics to keep pace with real-world advancements but also for managers to understand the increasing importance of dealing with patient engagement as a strategy that can positively impact healthcare organizations' efficiency.

2.2.2 Methodology

The research question driving the investigation in this chapter of the book calls for a systematic approach to investigate the current state of the art at the intersection between patient engagement and the impact of these strategies and approaches on healthcare organizations' efficiency.

First of all, it is fundamental to specify what do we mean when we talk about patient engagement and what we identify as healthcare organizations' efficiency. Patient engagement can be defined as the process of involving patients and their families as partners in their own healthcare (Graffigna & Barello, 2017). It includes informing patients, engaging them in decision-making, empowering them to take control of their health, and establishing a partnership with healthcare providers (Graffigna et al., 2017; Vrijhoef, 2015). The ultimate goal of patient engagement is to actively support patients in managing their health through various means such as education, communication, and shared decision-making (Dukhanin et al., 2018; Sagen et al., 2023).

Healthcare organizations' efficiency is defined as the ability to optimize health outcomes by efficiently utilizing the available resources (Gyrd-Hansen, 2014). This involves the strategic management of factors such as workforce and capital in order to enhance both the quality and the quantity of healthcare services provided (Cylus et al., 2016; Laurance et al., 2014). Efficiency plays a critical role in healthcare organizations by improving the delivery of patient care and satisfaction while effectively managing costs. It involves achieving technical, production, and allocative efficiency in delivering healthcare services, with a focus on enhancing health outcomes, reducing costs, and improving treatment effectiveness (Tehrani & Meckl-Sloan, 2016). Through the integration of behavioral and physical health services, healthcare organizations strive to progress towards value-based care, thereby aiming to reduce hospital admissions, minimize unnecessary emergency room visits, and improve overall healthcare provision to the community (Ramanuj et al., 2018).

Thus, the rationale for this methodological approach is rooted in the critical role that patient engagement plays in transforming healthcare outcomes and experiences. Although the positive impacts of patient engagement are widely recognized, there is a recognized gap that connects these strategies directly to improvements in healthcare organizational efficiency. This existing gap highlights the necessity of a systematic review, which can offer a first approach to reach a comprehensive and unbiased synthesis of the existing literature.

To address the research question, "How do patient engagement strategies impact healthcare organizations' process efficiency?", we employed the protocols of a systematic literature review (SLR) to comprehensively gather, evaluate, and synthesize relevant research while ensuring the findings are reported in a clear and systematic manner (Denyer & Tranfield, 2009; Tranfield et al., 2003). SLRs play a crucial role in the establishment of a robust knowledge foundation, the examination of essential management and research matters, and the identification of potential avenues for further exploration (Tranfield et al., 2003; Williams et al., 2021). This systematic methodology provides a well-organized and replicable procedure that efficiently handles the breadth of our research scope (Crossan & Apaydin, 2010; Tranfield et al., 2003).

Ensuring transparency throughout all stages of the SLR is fundamental to maintain its scientific quality, reliability, and reproducibility (Rousseau et al., 2008). Achieving such transparency involves thorough documentation and adherence to established protocols, which facilitate peer evaluation and the replication of the

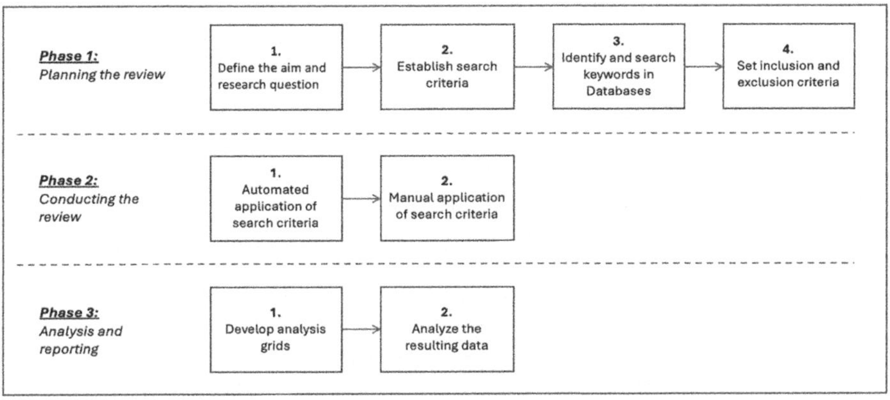

Fig. 2.1 The main phases of the systematic literature review (SLR). (*Source*: adapted from Denyer & Tranfield, 2009; Williams et al., 2021; Sanguineti et al., 2023)

study. This investigation adheres to recognized and broadly accepted SLR protocols (Denyer & Tranfield, 2009; Tranfield et al., 2003) to fulfill these rigorous criteria and maintain a methodical approach.

The review process is divided into three main stages, as depicted in Fig. 2.1: planning the review, conducting the review, and analyzing and reporting the outcomes. Each stage includes a sequence of steps crafted to systematically guide the research process. In the *planning stage*, the research aims and questions are explicitly outlined, and the criteria for study inclusion and exclusion are specified. Throughout the *conducting stage*, a thorough exploration of identified databases is conducted, followed by the selection and assessment of studies in line with the predetermined criteria. Ultimately, in the *analysis and reporting stage*, the data derived from the chosen studies are synthesized and the results thoroughly reported.

In the following sections, every stage of the systematic review process is comprehensively reported and explained. This methodical approach guarantees a systematic conduct of the review, providing significant perspectives on the influence of patient engagement strategies on healthcare organizations' efficiency.

Phase 1: Planning the Review

The initial phase of the review process concentrates on planning and consists of four essential steps, as shown in Fig. 2.1 and explained in Fig. 2.2. Once the primary objective of the study and the research question (RQ) "How do patient engagement strategies impact healthcare organizations' process efficiency?" are established, a set of keywords was identified. These keywords encompass two key concepts: patient engagement and healthcare organizations' process efficiency.

To carry out the search for the manuscripts, we opted for four well-known web-based databases: Google Scholar, PubMed, Scopus, and Web of Science (e.g.,

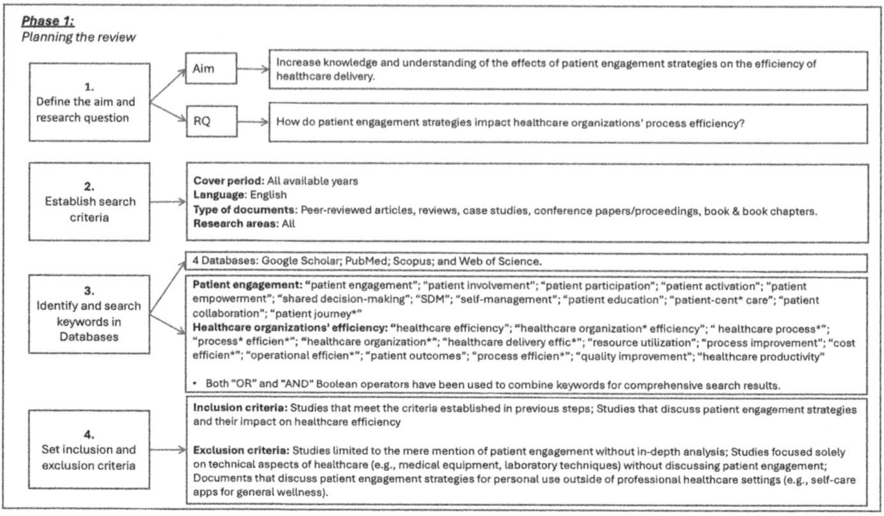

Fig. 2.2 First phase of the SLR—planning the review. (*Source*: adapted from Denyer & Tranfield, 2009; Williams et al., 2021; Sanguineti et al., 2023)

Hickmann et al., 2022; Jones et al., 2011). The choice of keywords, as shown in Fig. 2.2, was informed by a thorough examination of existing literature and aims to comprehensively address the research area. Keywords like "patient engagement," "healthcare organizations' efficiency," and related terms were combined using both "OR" and "AND" Boolean operators to facilitate an exhaustive exploration of their connections (Sanguineti et al., 2023).

Concerning the search criteria, our search was limited to publications in English but did not impose restrictions on publication timeframe, document type, source, or specific research field. This decision was made because patient engagement and healthcare organizations' process efficiency are topics that could be explored in various disciplines (i.e., healthcare, management, and economics) and publication genres, ensuring a wide and inclusive review of extant literature. Valuable insights on patient engagement may be found in both management journals and publications with a more clinical focus.

The final stage in the planning phase involved establishing specific inclusion and exclusion criteria, again summarized in Fig. 2.2. This step is fundamental in guaranteeing that all included documents are directly linked to the research question. We excluded articles that merely mention patient engagement without substantial analysis, those focused solely on too technical aspects of healthcare (e.g., case studies of one specific disease that could not be generalized to other areas), and documents discussing patient engagement strategies outside structured healthcare environments. This selective approach aims to maintain the focus and relevance of the review, laying a strong groundwork for the subsequent phases of the systematic literature review.

Phase 2: Conducting the Review

The second phase is dedicated to conducting the review (Denyer & Tranfield, 2009; Snyder, 2019; Tranfield et al., 2003) and involves two main steps as summarized in Fig. 2.3. The aim of this phase is to systematically collect and refine the studies intended for the final analysis, ensuring a thorough and reproducible selection process.

The first step involved an automatic application of the search criteria, applying the predefined keywords (refer to Phase 1 and Fig. 2.2) across the four mostly used academic online databases: Google Scholar, PubMed, Scopus, and Web of Science. This procedure aimed at identifying all published documents containing the specified keywords—with the assistance of "OR" and "AND" Boolean operators as previously mentioned—in their title, abstract, keywords, or body of the text. The initial pool of studies gathered from this search was 4876. Subsequently, duplicates were recognized and eliminated, resulting in 3298 unique studies for further assessment.

The second step required a careful manual application of the search criteria. Each study's abstract was individually examined by the author to ensure its relevance to the research questions. Two additional researchers were asked to double-check the selection for all documents included in the final database, not only those about which the main researcher was uncertain. This further step was crucial since the researchers realized that many initially identified studies could be only marginally related to the main research focus.

Chosen studies were those that directly covered the influence of patient engagement (strategies) on healthcare organizations' process efficiency. To streamline this

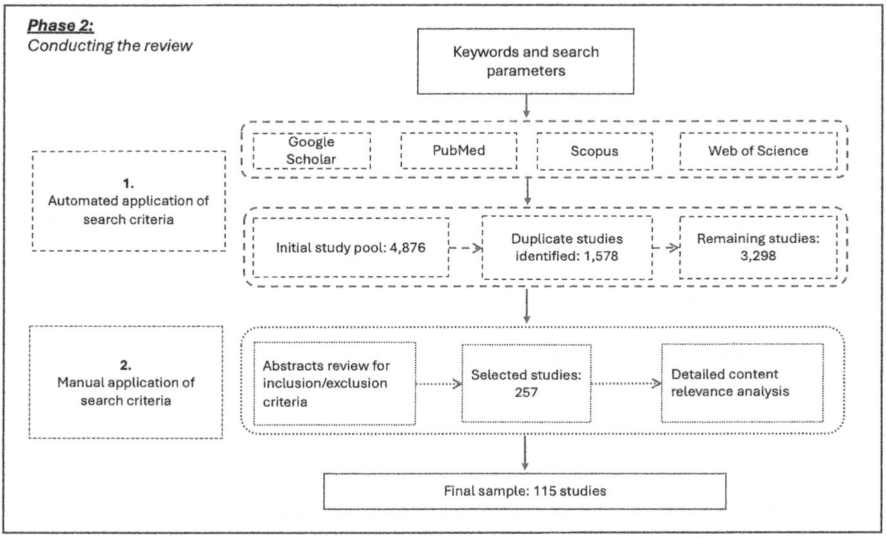

Fig. 2.3 Second phase of the SLR—conducting the review. (*Source*: adapted from Denyer & Tranfield, 2009; Williams et al., 2021; Sanguineti et al., 2023)

process, a preliminary classification was applied to the dataset, grouping documents under headings like "included," "out of scope," and "out of topic." Studies in the "included" group are those that directly investigate the influence of patient engagement on the efficiency of healthcare organizations' processes. These studies address the main research question and respond to the main inclusion criteria previously defined. For example, articles that assess the impact of shared decision-making or patient-centered care initiatives on hospital efficiency would fall into this category.

The "out of scope" group comprises studies that may touch on patient engagement or healthcare organizations' process efficiency but do not match the specific criteria outlined in the review's protocol first phase. For instance, studies exploring patient engagement in non-healthcare contexts such as community health programs or research on veterinary care would be considered out of scope given that the review concentrate solely on human healthcare within clinical setups.

Lastly, the group named "out of topic" includes studies that deviate significantly from the central themes of patient engagement and healthcare organizations' process efficiency. Among these, we have inserted research solely focused on medical equipment, healthcare policy adjustments that lack direct relevance to patient engagement, or studies that briefly mention patient engagement without offering in-depth analysis or pertinent outcomes. Such studies do not directly contribute to addressing the research question and therefore are excluded from further scrutiny.

Every remaining article underwent a full-text assessment to validate its relevance and contribution to the research question. This evaluation led to a refined selection of 257 studies considered suitable for an in-depth content relevance analysis. During this final step, the content of each study was thoroughly reviewed given that the prior selection was done only by reading and reviewing the abstracts. It helped ensuring that each study was properly aligned with the scope of the study while offering significant insights to respond to the research question. This step resulted in a final sample of 115 studies.

This approach based on a previously defined protocol (e.g., Denyer and Tranfield, 2009; Snyder, 2019; Tranfield et al., 2003) aims at guaranteeing that all studies included in the final sample are aligned with the study and contribute to comprehending the impacts of patient engagement on healthcare organizations' process efficiency. The result is a comprehensive body of literature that serves as the foundation for the next phases of the systematic literature review.

Phase 3: Analysis and Reporting

The third phase of the review process involved two main steps for analysis and reporting, as shown in Fig. 2.1 and then specified in Fig. 2.4. This phase initially includes creating two types of analysis grids using Microsoft Excel (Sanguineti et al., 2023). These grids are then used as bases for our analysis and interpretation.

The first one, the general grid, was crafted to include specific information about each document in our dataset, such as publication type, authors, title, publication year, research method, research design, and the abstract. This grid offers a

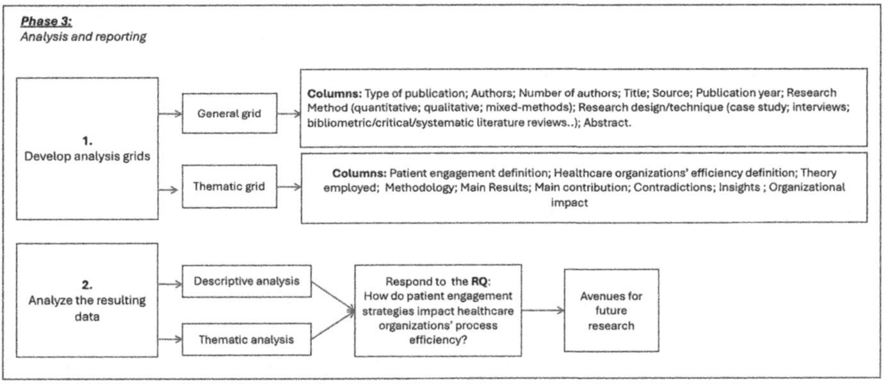

Fig. 2.4 Third phase of the SLR—analysis and reporting. (*Source*: adapted from Denyer & Tranfield, 2009; Williams et al., 2021; Sanguineti et al., 2023)

descriptive summary of the literature included in the review and, therefore, forms the basis for the descriptive analysis of the sample.

The other grid, the thematic one, was developed to extract and organize content directly related to our research question, including patient engagement definition, healthcare organizations' efficiency definition, theories used, methodology, main results, contributions, contradictions, insights, and organizational impact. This grid helped in identifying the variables driving the thematic investigation.

After completing the grids, the following step involved conducting a data analysis. This included both descriptive and thematic analysis techniques to understand how findings from different studies are linked and to draw conclusions regarding the impact of patient engagement on healthcare organizations' efficiency. Each analysis was done to start responding to the research question driving this chapter of the book: How do patient engagement impact healthcare organizations' process efficiency?

Through synthesizing the findings, we highlighted existing gaps in current literature. As a result of the SRL and drawing from the insights gained and gaps identified, we put forth a future research agenda aimed at exploring those under-investigated areas of research. We underscore the need to promote further empirical research that could offer deeper insights into maximizing patient engagement approaches to improve healthcare organizations' process efficiency.

2.3 Findings

The 115 studies investigated in this study suggest that patient engagement strategies can indeed influence healthcare organizations' process efficiency. The impacts of these approaches is evident both at the individual level, such as improving treatment adherence, and at the organization level, where reducing unnecessary procedures also minimizes costs to essentials (Marzban et al., 2022).

Before diving into the thematic analysis of the sample and start addressing the research question, we offer an overview of the current state of the art on the topic. The descriptive analysis supports in identifying what has been investigated and through which type of study.

2.3.1 *Current State of the Art*

The descriptive analysis used to take a snapshot of the current state of the art in terms of number of publications per year, type of journal outlets, or type of publications (i.e., qualitative studies, quantitative studies, or literature reviews) is based on the information reported in the general grid.

The interest in the research area, patient engagement strategies influence on healthcare organizations' process efficiency, has been steadily growing, reaching a pick of 23 published papers (please refer to Fig. 2.5 for details), which approximately represents the 19% of our sample, in 2022. The increase of interest in the years right after the pandemic might be strictly linked to the augmented focus on improving healthcare delivery and patient outcomes during a time of global health crisis. The pandemic has accelerated research and innovation in this field, as healthcare organizations were forced to find effective ways to engage patients remotely and manage resources more efficiently. The associated increase in publications underscores how critical is the role of patient engagement strategies in navigating the challenges exaggerated by the pandemic and destined to change the healthcare setting systems in the future.

The distribution of publication types in the sample further highlights the emerging nature and increasing interest in this research area. As shown in Fig. 2.6, the

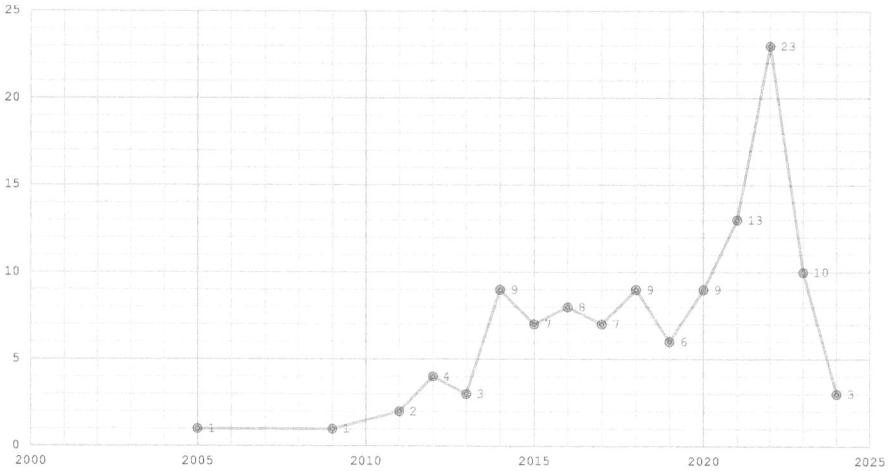

Fig. 2.5 Number of publications per year. *Source*: own elaboration

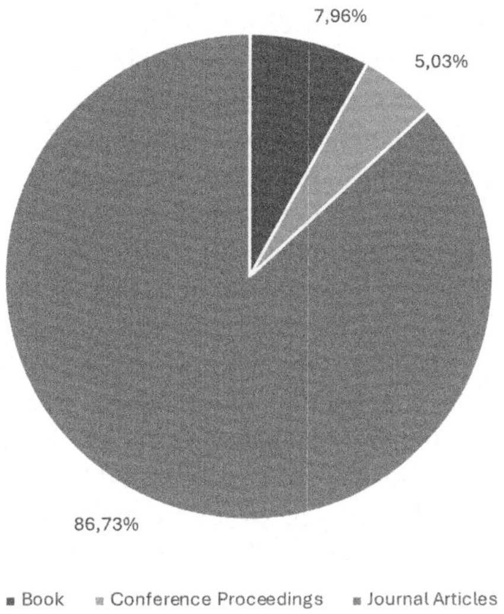

Fig. 2.6 Type of publications of the sampled manuscripts. *Source*: own elaboration

Table 2.1 Journal sources of the sampled articles

Journal	Papers
Health expectations	6 (5.41%)
BMJ open	4 (3.6%)
Research involvement and engagement	4 (3.6%)
Frontiers in psychology	3 (2.7%)

Source: own elaboration

majority of the publications are journal articles (86.73%), followed by a smaller proportion of books (7.96%) and conference proceedings (5.03%). This predominance of journal articles reflects the dissemination of research findings through peer-reviewed journals, which are considered high-impacting and widely accessible.

Thus, the significant share of journal articles suggests that the topic of patient engagement strategies in healthcare process efficiency is gaining importance in academic research. However, the presence of books and conference proceedings also indicates ongoing efforts to explore and discuss these strategies in broader formats and at academic conferences, which are platforms for sharing emerging research and encouraging academic discussions.

These manuscripts are all scattered across different journal outlets. In fact, only 15% of the 115 sampled manuscripts are published in 4 journals as summarized in Table 2.1, while the rest are all placed in different sources. Unsurprisingly, the majority of the studies investigating patient engagement are published in journals with a psychological or health expectation focus, rather than managerial journals. This distribution underscores a significant interdisciplinary interest, with a substantial contribution from the field of psychology. At the same time, we can already understand that studies investigating the managerial outcome of these strategies are strongly needed. If we are able to show that the baseline idea of improving patient engagement, at different levels, impacts the management of healthcare organizations, we could really contribute both in theory and, probably even more, in practice.

In fact, despite the managerial implications of improving patient engagement, only two manuscripts, both in 2022, are published in the Academy of Management Proceedings, and a few others are scattered across various management journals. This suggests that while there is growing interest in the managerial aspect of patient engagement, much still remains under-investigated. This highlights the complexity of patient engagement in healthcare organizations' process efficiency, suggesting a need for further integration of managerial insights into this research area.

Therefore, the outcome of Fig. 2.5, showing an increased interest in this research field, coupled with the sources in which these studies have been published, suggests that the topic is indeed of interest for both academics and practitioners. Yet, it also highlights the need to better address this theme in the managerial world, as multidisciplinary approaches are more and more needed to support healthcare organizations' efficiency. This is important to overcome the limitations of the system that became evident during the pandemic, but that must be addressed to ensure better outcomes for the entire healthcare system, both in the present and the future.

Another aspect that leads to thinking that, despite its well-known overall importance and its "trendy" concept, research investigating patient engagement impact on organizations' process efficiency is at its infancy is related to the type of approaches used by the identified sample. Table 2.2 shows that the 50% of the sample consists of conceptual studies or literature reviews and the other 50% is made of empirical studies, mostly focused on quantitative studies.

The significant proportion of literature reviews (25%) and conceptual studies (25%) suggests that the field is still developing. Literature reviews are often conducted to synthesize existing knowledge and identify gaps, providing a foundation for future research. Conceptual studies, which mostly focus on explaining constructs, are crucial for establishing theoretical frameworks and refining key concepts in an emerging field. The prevalence of these types of studies indicates that researchers are still in the process of building a comprehensive understanding of patient engagement and its implications for organizations' efficiency.

Table 2.2 Type of research approach adopted in the documents in the sample

Conceptual		*28(25%)*
Literature reviews		*30 (25%)*
	Systematic	14 (12%)
	Scoping	9 (7%)
	Narrative	6 (5%)
Empirical		*57 (50%)*
	Qualitative	14 (12%)
	Quantitative	36 (32%)
	Mixed methods	7 (6%)

Source: own elaboration

Yet, the fact that half of the studies (50%) are empirical, with a strong focus on quantitative surveys, underscores the growing recognition of the importance of this topic. These empirical studies demonstrate an active effort to gather data and evidence, particularly from patients' perspectives. This emphasis on empirical research highlights the practical relevance of patient engagement strategies and their potential to significantly impact healthcare outcomes. The focus on quantitative methods and patient surveys reflects the need to understand and measure the effectiveness of these strategies in real-world settings.

Therefore, the distribution of study approaches indicates that while patient engagement strategies in healthcare organizations' process efficiency is still emerging, it is already well recognized for its importance. The presence of substantial literature reviews and conceptual studies suggests that foundational work is still being laid, whereas the significant number of empirical studies highlights the practical importance and actual contribution of this specific topic. This underscores the need for continued research and collaboration to further develop and implement effective patient engagement strategies in healthcare.

Finally, most of the studies investigated are authored by less than five scholars as detailed in Fig. 2.7, which highlights the collaborative nature of research in this field. Yet, this pattern is not in line with what usually happens for medical studies, where larger author groups are more common. It seems to be more aligned with managerial studies, where smaller author teams are instead the norm. Thus, this might reflect the early stage of development in this research area within the managerial field.

Yet, the presence of studies with larger author groups suggests that there are also interdisciplinary collaborations that help bring together diverse perspectives. Such collaborations are fundamental for addressing patient engagement in its

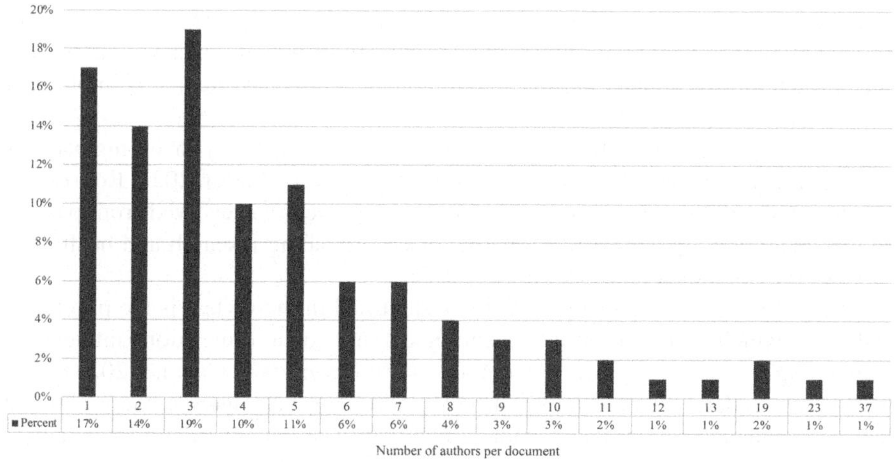

Fig. 2.7 Number of authors per document. *Source*: own elaboration

multifaceted nature, integrating insights from psychology, healthcare management, and other related fields.

Therefore, the descriptive analysis of the sample highlights an increased interest in patient engagement strategies and their impact on healthcare organizations' process efficiency, even if the managerial aspects are mostly overlooked. While patient engagement has been a recognized concept since 2005, its exploration within the context of organizational efficiency seems relatively new. An in-depth exploration of the general grid indicates that this research area is acknowledged for its importance, as evidenced by the growing number of publications and the interdisciplinary interest. However, the high number of literature reviews and conceptual studies suggests that foundational work is still being laid.

This underscores the need for further empirical investigation, with specific attention to managerial implications, to fully understand and implement effective patient engagement strategies that could positively impact healthcare organizations. To provide a more nuanced understanding of the current research landscape and identifying key areas for future exploration, we now move to the thematic analysis.

2.3.2 Main Research Streams

The analysis of the thematic grid helped in identifying the main research streams addressed by extant literature. These have been identified as (i) theoretical perspectives on patient engagement, (ii) patient engagement strategies, and (iii) integrating patient engagement with healthcare organizations' efficiency:

(i) *Theoretical perspectives on patient engagement*

The systematic literature review reveals diverse theoretical perspectives on patient engagement, reflecting its multifaceted nature and the various disciplines that investigate the topic. These perspectives range from psychosocial views to organizational studies, highlighting the complexity of patient engagement and the need for a multidisciplinary approach to fully understand and effectively implement it in healthcare settings.

Patient engagement is often described as a process of actively involving patients in their care, treatment plans, and health-related decisions (Porter, 2022; Rodríguez-Fuertes et al., 2023). The concept of patient engagement has evolved from passive endorsement and agreement to reshaping or co-producing research and healthcare services (Hickmann et al., 2022; Porter, 2022).

One of the key theoretical perspectives identified in the review is the psychosocial view, which emphasizes the psychological and social dimensions influencing patient engagement (e.g., Graffigna et al., 2020; Marino and Capone, 2024). This perspective underscores the importance of addressing both mental and emotional factors to enhance patient engagement effectively. The Patient Health Engagement model, for example, describes patient engagement as a developmental process, highlighting the integral role of psychological resilience and social support in fostering engagement (Graffigna & Barello, 2018a, b).

Another important theoretical perspective is the engagement capacity framework, which explores engagement facilitators, such as self-efficacy, resources, willingness, and capabilities (Sieck et al., 2022). This framework offers insights into how healthcare organizations can support patient engagement by considering the context of engagement and examining these precursors. The framework emphasizes the role of healthcare organizations in providing advice, tools, connection, and training to facilitate patient engagement and establish a strong partnership between patients and clinicians.

From an organizational studies perspective, some frameworks and models have been developed that aim to deepen the understanding of how patients can actively participate in their healthcare within organizations. The Patient Portal Engagement Framework, for example, categorizes engagement levels within patient portals, ranging from basic tasks to more complex activities that support a care ecology beyond hospital settings (Zhou et al., 2022). This framework highlights the evolving role of digital tools in facilitating patient engagement and promoting health literacy (Zhou et al., 2022).

The importance of system-level structures in facilitating patient engagement is also emphasized. A study on Twitter conversations around patient engagement hashtags aligns with the Strategy for Patient-Oriented Research – Patient Engagement framework (Canadian Institutes of Health Research, 2014) and introduces "impact" as a novel theme (Dunstan et al., 2023). This perspective overall underscores respect, support, collaboration, inclusivity, and impact as foundational pillars of meaningful patient engagement. Patients are seen as "active partners in health research" who should be involved in "key governance structures and decision-making processes" (Canadian Institute of Health Research - "Core Areas for Engagement", 2014). Another study highlights the significance of education, training, experience, and diversity among stakeholders as crucial elements for fostering a meaningful co-creation process in healthcare services (Sagen et al., 2023).

The professionalization of patient engagement representatives is examined through the lens of organizational legitimacy, influenced by democratic and technocratic rationales (Reid & Andiappan, 2022). This theoretical model helps understand how professionalization occurs and is sustained within healthcare organizations, and it emphasizes the balance between integrating patients as legitimate stakeholders in healthcare while maintaining professional standards.

In the context of online health communities, social support theory is applied to understand the mechanisms through which social support impacts patient engagement (Wang et al., 2023). This perspective illustrates how online communities can foster patient engagement by providing emotional and informational support, highlighting the roles of peer involvement and community status.

Finally, extant literature strongly emphasizes the importance of trust and collaborative relationships in patient-oriented research (Nicholls et al., 2022). This perspective shows how healthcare organizations could support and sustain patient engagement through trust-building actions and activities, underscoring the critical role of trust in fostering meaningful patient participation in research.

Therefore, the theoretical perspectives identified underscore the complexity of patient engagement and the need for a multidisciplinary approach to fully understand and effectively implement it in healthcare settings.

Patient Engagement Strategies

The second research stream resulting from the thematic analysis focuses on the various strategies employed by healthcare organizations to enhance patient engagement. These strategies aim to actively involve patients in their healthcare journey, improve health outcomes, and optimize the overall healthcare experience.

An identified important strategy is the integration of patient engagement functionalities into electronic health records (EHRs) (Upadhyay & Bhandari, 2022). The study found that patient engagement through EHR presence reduces readmission rates for certain diseases (i.e., acute myocardial infarction). This is supported also by other studies (i.e., Lobach et al., 2022) that explore, for instance, the integration of a patient engagement app into an electronic health record using interoperability standards, highlighting the potential of digital health tools to enhance patient engagement. This suggests that the collaboration and cooperation of patient engagement functionalities with EHR implementation can lead to improved health outcomes. Yet, in practice, much still need to be done before seeing this merge as a routinary approach.

Effective communication and collaboration between patients and healthcare providers are also crucial for successful patient engagement strategies. Strategies such as shared decision-making, motivational interviewing, and shared medical appointments have been identified as promising approaches to enhance patient involvement in their care (Easley et al., 2023; Miller-Rosales et al., 2022; Teo et al., 2022). These perspectives underscore the need for a mutual partnership between patients and healthcare professionals to achieve optimal engagement (Jerofke-Owen et al., 2023). However, the adoption of these strategies varies among physician practices, highlighting the need for further promotion and implementation at the organization level.

The literature also emphasizes the importance of patient-centered engagement, where patient communities are systematically integrated throughout the research and development process (Arntsen et al., 2022). This approach requires a strong commitment from all stakeholders and can lead to assessments that are more relevant to those directly affected by them. Patient education and empowerment are also key strategies for promoting patient engagement (Hickmann et al., 2022; Higgins et al., 2017). Providing patients with the necessary knowledge, skills, and resources to manage their own health can increase their self-efficacy as well as their motivation in following the clinicians' guidelines (Teo et al., 2022).

Finally, extant literature highlights the need for inclusive patient engagement processes to address health inequities and promote healthcare transformation (Snow,

2022). This involves considering factors such as gender, race, ability, sexual orientation, and other dimensions of diversity to create socially correct healthcare systems.

(ii) *Integrating patient engagement with healthcare organizations' process efficiency*

The literature review reveals a growing interest in integrating patient engagement strategies with healthcare organizations' process efficiency to improve overall performance, quality of care, and patient outcomes. This research stream emphasizes the importance of optimizing resource allocation, enhancing care quality, and promoting staff and patient satisfaction through the effective implementation of patient engagement strategies.

One of the key aspects explored in the literature is the incorporation of patients' experiences and emotions into healthcare organization management. Studies propose techniques to analyze patients' emotions during the care process and examine how these emotions influence their satisfaction (e.g., Marino and Capone, 2024; Rodríguez-Fuertes et al., 2023). The findings suggest that addressing patients' emotions and integrating psychosocial elements into value-based healthcare initiatives can improve the effectiveness of healthcare services and lead to better patient outcomes. However, the literature also highlights that there are not enough practical examples—or empirical studies—in this area, emphasizing the need for further research and implementation.

Another crucial aspect discussed in the literature is the intersection of patient engagement, social determinants of health, and healthcare equity in healthcare organizations. Studies report case studies and frameworks that emphasize the interconnectedness of these three domains (e.g., Sieck et al., 2022). By adopting an integrated approach to address patient engagement, social determinants of health, and health equity, healthcare organizations can pave the way towards equitable healthcare and improved efficiency. Extant literature underscores the importance of considering these factors as connected elements rather than isolated aspects of healthcare delivery.

The role of healthcare organizations in supporting a strong partnership between patients and clinicians through various mechanisms is also emphasized. Studies identify key functions of healthcare organizations, such as offering advice and support for patients, providing tools for communication, encouraging connection with patients, and training employees in cultural competency and communication skills (e.g., Lobach et al., 2022; Sieck et al., 2022). These mechanisms can facilitate patient engagement and enhance the patient-clinician relationship, with the final aim of improving healthcare efficiency. The literature also explores the use of interoperability standards, such as Health Level 7 Fast Healthcare Interoperability Resources, to integrate patient engagement apps into EHR-enabled workflows, highlighting the potential of these technologies to overcome barriers and improve efficiency (i.e., Upadhyay and Bhandari, 2022).

The effective utilization of lean interventions supported by digital technologies is another key aspect of healthcare organizations' efficiency. Studies have found that lean interventions combined with technologies such as simulation and automation lead to improved patient flow outcomes, including decreases in turnaround time, length of stay, and waiting time (i.e., Gualandi et al., 2020; Tlapa et al., 2022). These interventions also positively impact patient and staff satisfaction, highlighting the potential of lean practices and digital technologies to enhance organizations' efficiency.

The literature also emphasizes the significance of knowledge management in healthcare enterprises for efficient operations. Studies propose knowledge management platforms to address gaps in process-related knowledge management among healthcare facilities (e.g., Kushniruk et al., 2020; Solomon et al., 2022). By improving knowledge sharing and collaboration, healthcare organizations can optimize their processes and enhance overall efficiency.

Furthermore, the potential of remote care delivery models to efficiently support individuals with chronic conditions is underscored in the literature. Studies show high patient satisfaction, engagement, and clinical improvements in chronic patients using remote disease management solutions (Cadel et al., 2021; LoPresti et al., 2014; Pierz et al., 2024; Tehrani, 2015). The findings support the feasibility of using remote care models by combining technology with personalized care delivery. However, the literature also highlights the need for longitudinal studies to investigate the long-term effectiveness and efficiency of these solutions, which have just began to be implemented.

Therefore, the integration of patient engagement strategies with healthcare organizations' process efficiency is a complex and multifaceted area that requires addressing various interconnected aspects. The literature emphasizes the importance of incorporating patients' experiences and emotions, addressing social determinants of health and health equity, fostering strong patient-clinician partnerships, leveraging digital technologies, implementing lean interventions, improving knowledge management, and exploring remote care delivery models. By adopting a comprehensive approach that considers these elements, healthcare organizations should be able to improve overall efficiency, quality of care, and patient outcomes while promoting patient engagement and satisfaction. However, the literature also highlights the need for further research, practical implementation, and longitudinal studies to fully understand the impact and long-term effectiveness of these strategies.

2.4 Avenues for Future Research

The systematic literature review presented in this chapter provides insights into the current state of research on patient engagement strategies and their impact on healthcare organizations' process efficiency. While the review highlights the growing interest and importance of this topic, it also unveils several gaps and opportunities for future research, especially in the management field. Therefore, hereafter, we propose avenues for future research derived from the literature analysis. By addressing these areas, researchers can contribute to a more nuanced understanding of patient engagement and its potential to transform healthcare delivery:

(i) *Investigating patient engagement in the early stages of the patient journey*

One critical avenue for future research is the investigation of patient engagement strategies in the early stages of the patient journey. While existing literature emphasizes the importance of patient engagement throughout the healthcare process (Pierz et al., 2024; Porter, 2022), there is limited research specifically focusing on engagement during the initial phases, such as symptom recognition, appointment scheduling, or choice of the most appropriate care team. This gap in the literature presents an opportunity for researchers to explore how early engagement can influence patient outcomes, treatment adherence, and overall satisfaction with the healthcare experience.

Engaging patients in the early stages of their journey can have significant implications for healthcare organizations' process efficiency. For instance, effective communication and engagement during the front office operations, such as scheduling appointments and managing reservations, can ensure that patients feel valued and informed from their very first interaction. Moreover, by involving patients in decision-making processes from the outset, healthcare providers can ensure that treatment plans align with patients' values, preferences, and goals (Rodríguez-Fuertes et al., 2023). This alignment can lead to improved patient adherence, reduced healthcare costs, and better health outcomes (Marzban et al., 2022). Furthermore, early engagement can help identify potential barriers to treatment and enable healthcare providers to proactively address these challenges, enhancing the efficiency of care delivery. Future research should focus on developing and evaluating patient engagement strategies specifically tailored to the early stages of the patient journey, as well as examining the organizational factors that facilitate or hinder early engagement.

Linked to this, future studies could delve into the specific mechanisms through which early patient engagement affects subsequent stages of the patient journey. Understanding how initial interactions and decisions influence later stages, such as treatment adherence and follow-up care, can provide deeper insights into optimizing patient engagement. Researchers could investigate different types of engagement models and communication strategies to find which approaches are linked to the best outcomes for both the patients and the healthcare organizations. Comparative studies across different healthcare settings, such as primary care, emergency departments, and specialty clinics, can also reveal context-specific factors that impact engagement effectiveness. Therefore, future studies might be able to identify best practices while developing guidelines for healthcare providers to enhance early patient engagement and its positive effects on organization's process efficiency.

(ii) *Exploring the long-term impact of patient engagement strategies.*

Another important avenue for future research is the investigation of the long-term impact of patient engagement strategies on healthcare organizations' process efficiency. While existing studies have demonstrated the positive effects of patient engagement on various outcomes, such as treatment adherence, patient satisfaction, and healthcare costs (Alkhatib et al., 2024; Marzban et al., 2022), there is a lack of longitudinal research examining the sustainability and long-term effectiveness of these strategies (Cadel et al., 2021; Pierz et al., 2024).

To fully understand the potential of patient engagement to transform healthcare delivery, researchers should conduct longitudinal studies that assess the impact of engagement strategies over extended periods. These studies should investigate how patient engagement evolves over time, identifying factors that contribute to the sustainability of engagement and exploring the long-term effects on patient outcomes and healthcare organizations' efficiency. By examining the long-term impact, scholars could provide valuable insights linked to the effectiveness of different strategies and identify best practices for sustaining patient engagement over time. This research has the potential to lead to the development of patient engagement actions and strategies that are effective in the short term while also having the potential to drive lasting improvements in healthcare delivery.

Longitudinal research should also consider the role of patient demographics and specific characteristics in the long-term effectiveness of engagement strategies. Factors such as age, gender, and health literacy might influence how patients respond to engagement efforts over time. By considering these variables in longitudinal studies, scholars might gain a more comprehensive understanding of how patient engagement strategies can be personalized to different patient groups in order to maximize their effectiveness. Additionally, studies should explore the organizational—and systemic—changes needed to develop and support patient engagement, like training programs for healthcare provider or the integration of engagement tools into electronic health record systems.

Moreover, the economic implications of long-term patient engagement strategies is still an under investigated research area. While short-term benefits such as reduced readmission rates and increased patient satisfaction are attracting more and more academic and managerial attention, understanding the broader economic impact over time is fundamental for both healthcare organizations and policymakers. This might include, but is not limited to, cost savings from reduced emergency visits, potential improvement in preventive care, or better chronic disease management. By investigating and recognizing the potential long-term economic benefits of patient engagement strategies, future research can empirically demonstrate their potential to improve healthcare organizations' efficiency which, in turn, might not only positively impact the organization, but also—and probably even more—the individuals' lives and the overall healthcare system.

(iii) *Investigating the role of technology in facilitating patient engagement*

The rapid advancement of digital technologies has opened up new opportunities for patient engagement, yet the literature on the role of technology in facilitating this is still emerging. While some studies have explored the integration of patient engagement functionalities into, for instance, electronic health records or the use of mobile health applications (Lobach et al., 2022; Upadhyay & Bhandari, 2022), there is a need to further investigate how technology could be leveraged to enhance patient engagement in order to improve healthcare organizations' process efficiency.

Therefore, future research should investigate the design, implementation, and evaluation of technology-based patient engagement actions and strategies, such as patient portals or digital platforms, mobile health apps, and remote monitoring systems. Scholars should examine how these technologies can be properly integrated into existing healthcare processes and explore the barriers, drivers, and facilitators of their adoption and use. Moreover, studies should assess the impact of technology-based engagement strategies on both patient and organizational outcomes. Given that we are in an increasingly connected world, the actions taken by one organization might have an impact on the overall healthcare network and system. Investigating the adoption and usage of technologies that might positively affect patient engagement could yield even more interesting results when considering the possibilities for data collection and the significant impact this could have on the overall healthcare system and the optimization of resource allocation.

Future research should also take into consideration the user experience and accessibility of these technologies. It is important to understand how different patient groups, for example, those with diverse levels of digital literacy, interact with digital engagement tools. Investigating the potential barriers might also highlight strategies to overcome those. Therefore, studies should explore ways to make these technologies more inclusive and user-friendly, ensuring that all patient groups are properly targeted and health disparities not exacerbated. Furthermore, researchers should investigate the potential of emerging technologies, such as artificial intelligence or machine learning, to enhance patient engagement by providing personalized health recommendations.

Of course, the integration of digital health tools with traditional healthcare practices presents both challenges and opportunities. Future studies should examine how healthcare providers should be trained and supported to use these technologies effectively to enhance their daily practice. This includes, but it is not limited to, investigating the impact of digital tools on provider-patient communication, process efficiency, and overall care coordination.

(iv) *Examining the contextual and organizational factors influencing patient engagement*

While extant literature has identified various strategies for promoting patient engagement, there remains a need for further research on the contextual factors that influence the effectiveness of these strategies. Contextual factors, such as organizational culture, top management team's leadership, and resource availability, can significantly impact the implementation and success of patient engagement interventions (Jacob et al., 2022; Neuwirth, 2019; Sieck et al., 2022).

It would be important to examine how the design, implementation, and outcomes of patient engagement strategies is, or should be, shaped on the bases of these contextual factors. Therefore, studies should investigate the organizational characteristics that facilitate or hinder patient engagement, such as leadership commitment or staff training. Additionally, researchers should explore how patient engagement strategies can be tailored to different healthcare settings, such as primary care, specialty care, and community-based services.

Moreover, a culture that values patient-centered care and prioritizes patient engagement can significantly enhance the success of engagement initiatives. Therefore, investigating the influence of organizational culture on patient engagement is particularly important. Future studies should explore how organizational culture can be cultivated and sustained to support patient engagement efforts. A significant contribution to both theory and practice would arise if scholars could identify strategies for creating a culture that promotes patient engagement and aligns with organizational goals.

Finally, healthcare organizations have limited resources and may face challenges in adopting and implementing engagement actions. Therefore, resource availability is identified as another critical contextual factor that can affect the implementation of patient engagement strategies. Future studies should explore various approaches to resource allocation and management that can support patient engagement efforts, highlighting also its positive effects despite potential initial barriers. Among the features to be investigated, we identify the role of funding and funding sources, staff and training, and technological infrastructure that could facilitate engagement. Results from these studies should lead to the identification and development of best practices for resource management, through which scholars can provide practical recommendations for healthcare organizations in order to optimize their engagement strategies and improve overall efficiency.

(v) *Health equity and social determinants of health in patient engagement*

A further important avenue for future research appears to be the investigation of how patient engagement strategies can address health equity and social determinants of health. Existing literature has highlighted the importance of inclusive patient engagement processes to address health inequities and promote healthcare transformation (Sieck et al., 2022; Snow, 2022). However, how patient engagement interventions can be designed and implemented to effectively address these complex issues remain area ripe for further investigation.

Future research should examine how patient engagement strategies can be tailored to meet the needs of diverse patient populations, including those experiencing social and economic disadvantages. This is not only true in privatized healthcare systems; it is of fundamental importance in every world region. Studies should investigate the barriers to engagement faced by marginalized communities and explore approaches to overcoming, or at least reducing, these barriers. Additionally, studies should assess the impact of patient engagement interventions on health equity outcomes, such as access to care, quality of care, and health disparities. In this way, scholars have the chance to contribute to the development of more inclusive and equitable healthcare systems that prioritize the needs and perspectives of all patients.

Exploring the area of research at the intersection of patient engagement and social determinants of health requires a multidisciplinary approach that incorporates insights from various disciplines (i.e., public health, sociology, and healthcare management). Future studies should investigate how factors such as income, education, and transportation might influence patient engagement and health outcomes.

This would help in developing specific tactics or strategies aiming at reducing the causes of health disparities and promoting equity in healthcare.

The integration of health equity considerations into patient engagement strategies also involves evaluating the effectiveness of these interventions in diverse healthcare settings. An approach would be to conduct comparative analyses across different healthcare systems and world regions to identify best practices for promoting equity. This includes investigating the impact of policy interventions and healthcare reforms on patient engagement and health equity.

2.5 Conclusions

This chapter presented a systematic literature review to provide a comprehensive overview of the current state of research on patient engagement strategies and their impact on healthcare organizations' efficiency.

The review has revealed a growing interest in this topic, with an increasing number of publications in recent years, particularly after the COVID-19 pandemic. The majority of the studies are published in journals focusing on psychology and health expectations, highlighting the interdisciplinary nature of the research area. However, the managerial implications of patient engagement strategies remain under-investigated, emphasizing the need for further research in this domain.

The thematic analysis of the literature identifies three main research streams: (i) theoretical perspectives on patient engagement, (ii) patient engagement strategies, and (iii) integrating patient engagement with healthcare organizations' efficiency. The theoretical perspectives underscore the complexity of patient engagement and the need for a multidisciplinary approach to fully understand and effectively implement it in healthcare settings. The literature also explores various strategies employed by healthcare organizations to enhance patient engagement, such as the integration of patient engagement functionalities into electronic health records, effective communication and collaboration between patients and healthcare providers, and patient-centered engagement processes.

It is then highlighted the growing interest in integrating patient engagement strategies with healthcare organizations' efficiency to improve overall performance, quality of care, and patient outcomes. Key aspects explored in the literature include the incorporation of patients' experiences and emotions into healthcare organization management; the intersection of patient engagement, social determinants of health, and healthcare equity; and the role of healthcare organizations in supporting strong patient-clinician partnerships. The literature also emphasizes the potential of lean interventions, digital technologies, knowledge management, and remote care delivery models to enhance healthcare efficiency while promoting patient engagement.

Based on the identified gaps and opportunities in the current literature, the review proposes several avenues for future research. These include investigating patient engagement in the early stages of the patient journey, exploring the long-term impact of patient engagement strategies, examining the role of technology in facilitating patient engagement, analyzing the contextual factors influencing patient engagement, and addressing health equity and social determinants of health in patient engagement research. By pursuing these research directions, scholars can contribute to a more nuanced understanding of patient engagement and its potential to transform healthcare delivery, ultimately leading to improved patient outcomes and healthcare organizations' efficiency.

The next chapter of this book will present a case study of Fondazione Mondino Scientific Institutes for Research, Hospitalization, and Healthcare (IRCCS—Istituto di Ricovero e Cura a Carattere Scientifico), a renowned neurological hospital and research center in Italy, ranked among the top specialized hospitals globally (Statista, 2024). This case study will provide valuable insights into how patient engagement strategies are implemented in a real-world healthcare setting, offering a practical perspective on—some of—the findings of this systematic literature review. By examining the experiences and practices of Fondazione Mondino, the case study will showcase the challenges, opportunities, and benefits of integrating patient engagement strategies into healthcare organizations' operations processes. This practical application is a first attempt to start bridging the gap between theory and practice, aiming to raise managers' awareness of the increasing importance that patient engagement has from the point of view of the different stakeholders involved.

References

Alharbi, T. S. J., Carlström, E., Ekman, I., Jarneborn, A., & Olsson, L. E. (2014). Experiences of person-centred care-patients' perceptions: Qualitative study. *BMC Nursing, 13*, 1–9.

Alkhatib, A. J., AlZoubi, A., Alharoun, M., Aqoulah, A. A., & Mandili, A. (2024). The impact of patient engagement on healthcare: A systematic review of unveiling the benefits of patient engagement in healthcare. *Multicriteria Algorithms with Applications, 3*, 23–31.

Arntsen, K. A., Blount, L. G., Dickerson, B. J., Koola, C. P., Venable, Y., & Wildman, P. (2022). Patient-centered health technology assessment: A perspective on engagement in health technology assessment by three patient organizations and a health technology assessment body. *International Journal of Technology Assessment in Health Care, 38*(1), e76.

Barello, S., Graffigna, G., & Vegni, E. (2012). Patient engagement as an emerging challenge for healthcare services: Mapping the literature. *Nursing Research and Practice, 2012*.

Bertakis, K. D., & Azari, R. (2011). Patient-centered care is associated with decreased health care utilization. *The Journal of the American Board of Family Medicine, 24*(3), 229–239.

Bertorello, D., Brichetto, G., Folkvord, F., Theben, A., & Zaratin, P. (2022). A systematic review of patient engagement experiences in brain disorders. *Patient Related Outcome Measures*, 259–272.

Bombard, Y., Baker, G. R., Orlando, E., Fancott, C., Bhatia, P., Casalino, S., Onate, K., Denis, J.-L., & Pomey, M. P. (2018). Engaging patients to improve quality of care: A systematic review. *Implementation Science, 13*, 1–22.

Byrne, A. L., Baldwin, A., & Harvey, C. (2020). Whose Centre is it anyway? Defining person-centred care in nursing: An integrative review. *PLoS One, 15*(3), e0229923. https://doi.org/10.1371/journal.pone.0229923. PMID: 32155182; PMCID: PMC7064187.

Cadel, L., Marcinow, M., Sandercock, J., Dowedoff, P., Guilcher, S. J., Maybee, A., Law, S., & Kuluski, K. (2021). A scoping review of patient engagement activities during COVID-19: More consultation, less partnership. *PLoS One, 16*(9), e0257880.

Canadian Institutes of Health Research. (2014). Strategy for patient-oriented research: patient engagement framework. *Canadian Institutes of Health Research. Strategy for Patient-Oriented Research-Patient Engagement Framework-CIHR*. https://cihr-irsc.gc.ca/e/48413.html#a7

Carman, K. L., Dardess, P., Maurer, M., Sofaer, S., Adams, K., Bechtel, C., & Sweeney, J. (2013). Patient and family engagement: A framework for understanding the elements and developing interventions and policies. *Health Affairs, 32*(2), 223–231.

Chase, D. (2012). Patient engagement is the blockbuster drug of the century. Retrieved at: https://www.forbes.com/sites/davechase/2012/09/09/patient-engagement-is-the-blockbuster-drug-of-the-century/?sh=624d1ba45638. Accessed: 09.05.24.

Crossan, M. M., & Apaydin, M. (2010). A multi-dimensional framework of organizational innovation: A systematic review of the literature. *Journal of Management Studies, 47*(6), 1154–1191. https://doi.org/10.1111/j.1467-6486.2009.00880.x

Ćwiklicki, M., Klich, J., & Chen, J. (2020). The adaptiveness of the healthcare system to the fourth industrial revolution: A preliminary analysis. *Futures, 122*, 102602.

Cylus, J., Papanicolas, I., & Smith, P. C. (Eds.). (2016). *Health system efficiency: How to make measurement matter for policy and management*. European Observatory on Health Systems and Policies.

Daack-Hirsch, S., & Campbell, C. A. (2014). The role of patient engagement in personalized healthcare. *Personalized Medicine, 11*(1), 1–4. https://doi.org/10.2217/pme.13.102

Denyer, D., & Tranfield, D. (2009). Producing a systematic review. In *The SAGE handbook of organizational research methods* (pp. 671–689). Sage.

Dukhanin, V., Topazian, R., & DeCamp, M. (2018). Metrics and evaluation tools for patient engagement in healthcare organization-and system-level decision-making: A systematic review. *International Journal of Health Policy and Management, 7*(10), 889.

Dunstan, B., Buchanan, F., Maybee, A., Lofters, A., & Sayani, A. (2023). #HowNotToDoPatientEngagement: The engaging with purpose patient engagement framework based on a twitter analysis of community perspectives on patient engagement. *Research Involvement and Engagement, 9*(1), 119.

Easley, J., Wassersug, R., Matthias, S., Tompson, M., Schneider, N. D., O'Brien, M. A., Vick, B., & Fitch, M. (2023). Patient engagement in health research: Perspectives from patient participants. *Current Oncology, 30*(3), 2770–2780.

Engle, R. L., Mohr, D. C., Holmes, S. K., Seibert, M. N., Afable, M., Leyson, J., & Meterko, M. (2021). Evidence-based practice and patient-centered care: Doing both well. *Health Care Management Review, 46*(3), 174–184.

Graffigna, G., & Barello, S. (2017). The value of measuring patient engagement in healthcare: New frontiers for healthcare quality. In *Health literacy: Breakthroughs in research and practice* (pp. 392–414). IGI Global.

Graffigna, G., & Barello, S. (2018a). Patient health engagement (PHE) model in enhanced recovery after surgery (ERAS): Monitoring patients' engagement and psychological resilience in minimally invasive thoracic surgery. *Journal of Thoracic Disease, 10*(Suppl 4), S517.

Graffigna, G., & Barello, S. (2018b). Spotlight on the patient health engagement model (PHE model): A psychosocial theory to understand people's meaningful engagement in their own health care. *Patient Preference and Adherence*, 1261–1271.

Graffigna, G., Barello, S., Riva, G., & Bosio, C. (2014). Patient engagement: The key to redesign the exchange between the demand and supply for healthcare in the era of active ageing. *Active Ageing and Healthy Living: A Human Centered Approach in Research and Innovation as Source of Quality of Life, 203*, 85.

Graffigna, G., Barello, S., Riva, G., Savarese, M., Menichetti, J., Castelnuovo, G., & Bosio, A. C. (2017). Fertilizing a patient engagement ecosystem to innovate healthcare: Toward the first Italian consensus conference on patient engagement. *Frontiers in Psychology, 8*, 812.

Graffigna, G., Barello, S., Riva, G., Corbo, M., Damiani, G., Iannone, P., & Ricciardi, W. (2020). Italian consensus statement on patient engagement in chronic care: Process and outcomes.

International Journal of Environmental Research and Public Health, 17(11), 4167. https://doi.org/10.3390/ijerph17114167

Gualandi, R., Masella, C., & Tartaglini, D. (2020). Improving hospital patient flow: A systematic review. *Business Process Management Journal, 26*(6), 1541–1575.

Gyrd-Hansen, D. (2014). *Concepts of efficiency in health care. Encyclopedia of health economics*. Elsevier. https://doi.org/10.1016/B978-0-12-375678-7.00202-9

Hickmann, E., Richter, P., & Schlieter, H. (2022). All together now–patient engagement, patient empowerment, and associated terms in personal healthcare. *BMC Health Services Research, 22*(1), 1116.

Higgins, T., Larson, E., & Schnall, R. (2017). Unraveling the meaning of patient engagement: A concept analysis. *Patient Education and Counseling, 100*, 30–36.

Irizarry, T., DeVito Dabbs, A., & Curran, C. R. (2015). Patient portals and patient engagement: A state of the science review. *Journal of Medical Internet Research, 17*(6), e148.

Ivany, C., Hudson, T., Schneider, P., Farrukh, H., Swinton, M., & Ghert, M. (2023). Patient engagement in research; benefits, challenges, importance, and implications. *medRxiv*, 2023–2003.

Jacob, C., Bourke, S., & Heuss, S. (2022). From testers to cocreators—The value of and approaches to successful patient engagement in the development of eHealth solutions: Qualitative expert interview study. *JMIR Human Factors, 9*(4), e41481.

Jerofke-Owen, T. A., Tobiano, G., & Eldh, A. C. (2023). Patient engagement, involvement, or participation—Entrapping concepts in nurse-patient interactions: A critical discussion. *Nursing Inquiry, 30*(1), e12513.

Jones, M. V., Coviello, N., & Tang, Y. K. (2011). International entrepreneurship research (1989-2009): A domain ontology and thematic analysis. *Journal of Business Venturing, 26*(6), 632–659. https://doi.org/10.1016/j.jbusvent.2011.04.001

Krist, A. H., Tong, S. T., Aycock, R. A., & Longo, D. R. (2017). Engaging patients in decision-making and behavior change to promote prevention. *Information Services & Use, 37*(2), 105–122.

Kushniruk, A. W., Borycki, E. M., & Parush, A. (2020). A case study of patient journey mapping to identify gaps in healthcare: Learning from experience with cancer diagnosis and treatment. *Knowledge Management & E-Learning, 12*(4), 405.

Laurance, J., Henderson, S., Howitt, P. J., Matar, M., Al Kuwari, H., Edgman-Levitan, S., & Darzi, A. (2014). Patient engagement: Four case studies that highlight the potential for improved health outcomes and reduced costs. *Health Affairs, 33*(9), 1627–1634.

Li, C., Wang, J., Wang, S., & Zhang, Y. (2023). A review of IoT applications in healthcare. *Neurocomputing, 127017.*

Lobach, D. F., Boxwala, A., Kashyap, N., Heaney-Huls, K., Chiao, A. B., Rafter, T., Lomotan, E. A., Harrison, M., Dymek, C., Swiger, J., & Dullabh, P. (2022). Integrating a patient engagement app into an electronic health record-enabled workflow using interoperability standards. *Applied Clinical Informatics, 13*(05), 1163–1171.

LoPresti, M., Appelboom, G., Bruyère, O., Reginster, J. Y., Klug, E., & Connolly, E. S., Jr. (2014). Patient engagement in clinical research through mobile technology. *Clinical Practice, 11*(6), 549.

Marino, L., & Capone, V. (2024). Psychosocial factors contributing to value creation in value-based healthcare: A scoping review. *Frontiers in Psychology, 15*, 1323110. https://doi.org/10.3389/fpsyg.2024.1323110. PMID: 38655221; PMCID: PMC11036338.

Marzban, S., Najafi, M., Agolli, A., & Ashrafi, E. (2022). Impact of patient engagement on healthcare quality: A scoping review. *Journal of Patient Experience, 9*, 23743735221125439.

Merker, V. L., Hyde, J. K., Herbst, A., Solch, A. K., Mohr, D. C., Gaj, L., Dvorin, K., & Dryden, E. M. (2022). Evaluating the impacts of patient engagement on health services research teams: Lessons from the veteran consulting network. *Journal of General Internal Medicine, 37*(Suppl 1), 33–41.

Miller, K. L. (2016). Patient centered care: A path to better health outcomes through engagement and activation. *NeuroRehabilitation, 39*(4), 465–470.

Miller-Rosales, C., Miake-Lye, I. M., Brewster, A. L., Shortell, S. M., & Rodriguez, H. P. (2022). Pathways for primary care practice adoption of patient engagement strategies. *Health Services Research, 57*(5), 1087–1093.

Neuwirth, Z. E. (2019). *Reframing healthcare: A roadmap for creating disruptive change*. Advantage.

Nicholls, S. G., Fox, G., Monfaredi, Z., Poole, E., Garritty, C., Maybee, A., Presseau, J., Shea, B., & Fergusson, D. A. (2022). The impact of patient engagement on trials and trialists in Ontario, Canada: An interview study with IMPACT awardees. *Research Involvement and Engagement, 8*(1), 50.

Pierz, K. A., Locantore, N., McCreary, G., Calvey, R. J., Hackney, N., Doshi, P., Linnell, J., Sundaramoorthy, A., Reed, C. R., & Yates, J. (2024). Investigation of the impact of Wellinks on the quality of life and clinical outcomes in patients with chronic obstructive pulmonary disease: Interventional research study. *JMIR Formative Research, 8*, e47555.

Porter, L. D. (2022). The importance of patient engagement to improve healthcare research and safety. *Global Journal on Quality and Safety in Healthcare, 5*(2), 27–30.

Ramanuj, P. P., Scharf, D. M., Ferenchick, E., Spaeth-Rublee, B., & Pincus, H. A. (2018). Measuring efficiency at the Interface of behavioral and physical health care. *The Journal of Mental Health Policy and Economics, 21*(2), 79–86.

Reid, M., & Andiappan, M. (2022). Sustaining patient engagement professionalization through legitimacy. In *Academy of management proceedings* (Vol. 1, p. 14856). Academy of Management. https://doi.org/10.5465/AMBPP.2022.14856abstract

Rieckmann, P., Boyko, A., Centonze, D., Elovaara, I., Giovannoni, G., Havrdová, E., Hommes, O., Kesselring, J., Kobelt, G., Langdon, D., LeLorier, J., Morrow, S. A., Oreja-Guevara, C., Schippling, S., Thalheim, C., Thompson, H., & Vermersch, P. (2015). Achieving patient engagement in multiple sclerosis: A perspective from the multiple sclerosis in the 21st century steering group. *Multiple Sclerosis and Related Disorders, 4*(3), 202–218.

Rodríguez-Fuertes, A., Reinares-Lara, P., & Garcia-Henche, B. (2023). Incorporation of the emotional indicators of the patient journey into healthcare organization management. *Health Expectations, 26*(1), 297–306.

Rousseau, D. M., Manning, J., & Denyer, D. (2008). 11: Evidence in management and organizational science: Assembling the Field's full weight of scientific knowledge through syntheses. *The Academy of Management Annals, 2*(1), 475–515. https://doi.org/10.5465/19416520802211651

Sagen, J. S., Smedslund, G., Simonsen, A. E., Habberstad, A., Kjeken, I., Dagfinrud, H., & Moe, R. H. (2023). Patient engagement in the development and delivery of healthcare services: A systematic scoping review. *BMJ Open Quality, 12*(2), e002309.

Sanguineti, F., Magnani, G., & Zucchella, A. (2023). Technology adoption, global value chains and sustainability: The case of additive manufacturing. *Journal of Cleaner Production, 408*, 137095.

Saut, A. M., Ho, L. L., Berger, S., & Berssaneti, F. T. (2023). How did healthcare professionals define patient engagement in quality management? A survey study. *BMC Health Services Research, 23*(1), 173.

Schoenfeld, E. M., Goff, S. L., Elia, T. R., Khordipour, E. R., Poronsky, K. E., Nault, K. A., Lindenauer, P. K., & Mazor, K. M. (2016). The physician-as-stakeholder: An exploratory qualitative analysis of physicians' motivations for using shared decision making in the emergency department. *Academic Emergency Medicine, 23*(12), 1417–1427.

Sieck, C. J., Nicks, S. E., Salem, J., DeVos, T., Thatcher, E., & Hefner, J. L. (2022). Addressing equity and social needs: The new frontier of patient engagement research. In *Responding to the grand challenges in health care via organizational innovation* (Vol. 21, pp. 151–165). Emerald Publishing Limited.

Snow, M. E. (2022). Patient engagement in healthcare planning and evaluation: A call for social justice. *The International Journal of Health Planning and Management, 37*, 20–31.

Snyder, H. (2019). Literature review as a research methodology: An overview and guidelines. *Journal of business research, 104*, 333–339. https://doi.org/10.1016/j.jbusres.2019.07.039

Solomon, L., Gudi, R. B., Asfandiyar, H., Sneha, S., & Shahria, H. (2022). Knowledge Management in a Healthcare Enterprise: Creation of a digital knowledge repository. In *2022 IEEE international conference on digital health (ICDH)* (pp. 215–217). IEEE.

Statista. (2024). World's Best Specialized Hospitals 2023 by Newsweek. https://www.newsweek.com/rankings/worlds-best-specialized-hospitals-2023/neurology

Tehrani, N. (2015). Patient engagement in digital healthcare. *Innovative Journal of Medical and Health Science, 5*(2), 37–38. https://doi.org/10.15520/ijmhs.2015.vol5.iss2.50.37-38

Tehrani, N., & Meckl-Sloan, C. (2016). Patient engagement meets personalized interactive communication and the 3P's: Patients, providers and payers. *International Journal of Scientific and Research Publications, 6*(5).

Teo, J. L., Zheng, Z., & Bird, S. R. (2022). Identifying the factors affecting 'patient engagement'in exercise rehabilitation. *BMC Sports Science, Medicine and Rehabilitation, 14*(1), 18.

Tlapa, D., Tortorella, G., Fogliatto, F., Kumar, M., Mac Cawley, A., Vassolo, R., Enberg, L., & Baez-Lopez, Y. (2022). Effects of lean interventions supported by digital technologies on healthcare services: A systematic review. *International Journal of Environmental Research and Public Health, 19*(15), 9018.

Tranfield, D., Denyer, D., & Smart, P. (2003). Towards a methodology for developing evidence-informed management knowledge by means of systematic review. *British Journal of Management, 14*(3), 207–222. https://doi.org/10.1111/1467-8551.00375

Upadhyay, S., & Bhandari, N. (2022). Do patient engagement functionalities impact quality outcomes? The mediating role of EHR presence. In *Academy of management proceedings* (Vol. 1, p. 12220). Academy of Management. https://doi.org/10.5465/AMBPP.2022.12220abstract

Van den Borne, H. W. (1998). The patient from receiver of information to informed decision-maker. *Patient Education and Counseling, 34*(2), 89–102.

Vrijhoef, H. J. (2015). Patient engagement is the new hard currency in health care. *International Journal of Care Coordination, 18*(1), 3–4.

Wang, J., Yao, T., & Wang, Y. (2023). Patient engagement as contributors in online health communities: The mediation of peer involvement and moderation of community status. *Behavioral Sciences, 13*(2), 152.

Williams, R. I., Clark, L. A., Clark, W. R., & Raffo, D. M. (2021). Re-examining systematic literature review in management research: Additional benefits and execution protocols. *European Management Journal, 39*(4), 521–533. https://doi.org/10.1016/j.emj.2020.09.007

World Health Organization. (2016). *Patient engagement: Technical series on safer primary care. Geneva*. https://www.who.int/publications/i/item/9789241511629

Zhou, J., Arriaga, R. I., Liu, H., & Huang, M. (2022). A tale of two perspectives: Harvesting system views and user views to understand patient portal engagement. In *2022 IEEE 10th international conference on healthcare informatics (ICHI)* (pp. 373–383). IEEE.

Chapter 3
Fondazione Mondino IRCCS: A Case of Italian Excellence

Abstract Fondazione Mondino IRCCS exemplifies Italian excellence in neurological care, research, and education. Situated in Lombardy, a pivotal region in Italy's healthcare system, this institution integrates patient-centered care, cutting-edge research, and specialized education. Recognized among the world's top specialized hospitals for neurology, the institution reflects over a century of dedication to advancing neurological care. Designated as an IRCCS in 1973, it combines state-of-the-art clinical care with groundbreaking research and training, fostering strong ties with the University of Pavia. This chapter conceptualizes the foundation within Italy's healthcare system and Lombardy's regional prominence, highlighting its global influence and role as a leader in neurological science.

3.1 Introduction

In the landscape of neurological care and research, certain institutions emerge as pioneers, continuously pushing the boundaries of medical science while prioritizing patient well-being. Fondazione Mondino, situated in the historic city of Pavia, Italy, is a good example of such an institution. Its century-long commitment to advancing neuroscience has not only shaped its local community but has also earned its recognitions worldwide.

The recent World's Best Specialized Hospital 2023 (Statista, 2024) survey highlighted Fondazione Mondino's excellence. This evaluation resulting from a collaboration with Statista Inc. drew insights from 40,000 medical professionals worldwide. The survey aimed at evaluating specialized hospitals across 11 disciplines, with Fondazione Mondino ranking the 51st position—globally—in neurology. This achievement is particularly noteworthy when considering the weight of the other institutions included in the list.

At top was the Mayo Clinic in Rochester, USA, setting an extremely high benchmark for global excellence. Among Italian institutions, Fondazione Mondino found itself alongside the Carlo Besta Institute in Milan (ranked 11th), the Gemelli Polyclinic in Rome (33rd), and the San Raffaele Hospital in Milan (38th). This

F. Sanguineti, *The Organizational Impact of Patient Engagement*,
SpringerBriefs in Business, https://doi.org/10.1007/978-3-031-77964-0_3

recognition not only further underlined Fondazione Mondino's status as a leader in neurological care in Italy but also underscored its growing influence internationally.

The journey of Fondazione Mondino to this global recognition is rooted in its rich history. Founded in the early twentieth century, the institution has evolved from a local neurological clinic into a comprehensive center of excellence. Today, it integrates innovative research, specialized clinical care, and advanced medical education.

Fondazione Mondino is proof of the transformative power of putting patients first. With a team of over 400 dedicated professionals, including physicians, researchers, nurses, and support staff, the institution has crafted a comprehensive ecosystem of care that spans across its hospital, outpatient clinics, and day center. This multidisciplinary approach ensures that patients with a wide range of neurological conditions receive the highest quality of care, tailored to their needs and preferences.

However, before exploring the various strategies at the patient level implemented by Fondazione Mondino, it is of utmost importance to understand the case itself. Therefore, this chapter presents the context in which this healthcare organization operates, offering an overview of the Italian National Health Service and the specifics of the Scientific Institutes for Research, Hospitalization, and Healthcare (IRCCS), with a focus on the importance of the Lombardy region in the Italian healthcare system. Then, we comprehensively present Fondazione Mondino, which is not only an excellence in the Lombardy region but a leading institution for neurological research, clinical care, and education in Italy, renowned worldwide.

3.2 Institutional and Geographic Context

The Italian National Health Service (Servizio Sanitario Nazionale (SSN)) has been an essential element of the Italian welfare state since its establishment in 1978 (Legge 23 dicembre 1978, n.833). Founded on the principles of universalism, solidarity, and equity of access to benefits and services (Bachelet, 2008), the SSN has been fundamental in improving the health and well-being of the Italian population. However, the system has faced numerous challenges over the years, including financial constraints, regional disparities, and the need to adapt to an evolving aging demographic and epidemiological landscape (France et al., 2005).

3.2.1 The History of the Italian National Healthcare System

The origins of the Italian National Health Service (SSN) can be traced back to the mutual aid societies that emerged in the nineteenth century. These organizations, known as "società di mutuo soccorso," provided their members with financial support in case of illness, disability, or even death of the family member (Broek et al., 2012). As the industrial revolution progressed and the working class grew, these mutual aid societies became increasingly important in ensuring access to healthcare for a large portion of the Italian population (Tulchinsky & Varavikova, 2014).

In the early twentieth century, the Italian government began to take a more active role in the provision of healthcare services. The establishment of the national fund for disability and old age for workers—cassa nazionale di previdenza per l'invalidità e la vecchiaia degli operai—in 1898 marked the beginning of a national health insurance system. In 1933, this fund was transformed into the National Fascist Institute of Social Insurance—istituto nazionale fascista della previdenza sociale -, a public entity with legal personality and management autonomy (INPS, 2022). Finally, in 1944, it assumed its current name, the National Institute for Social Insurance (Istituto Nazionale della Previdenza Sociale, INPS) (Ricciardi & Tarricone, 2021). Over the following decades, various occupational health insurance funds were established, covering different categories of workers and their families.

Before the establishment of the SSN, Italy suffered a period of intense political and social upheaval. The 1970s were marked by a wave of labor unrest, student protests, and terrorist attacks, which highlighted the need for a more inclusive and responsive welfare state (Ricciardi & Tarricone, 2021). Setting up the SSN was part of a broader process of social and institutional reform that sought to address the inequalities and inefficiencies of the existing system. It was not until 1978 that the Italian National Health Service (SSN) was formally established through Law 833/1978. This landmark legislation aimed to create a universal, comprehensive, and equitable healthcare system, replacing the fragmented network of occupational health insurance funds. The SSN was modeled after the British National Health Service and was based on the principles of solidarity, universality, and equality (Ministero della Salute, 2019a).

Under the SSN, all Italian citizens and legal foreign residents were granted the right to access healthcare services free of charge. The system was financed through general taxation, with resources allocated to the regions based on a per capita formula adjusted for demographic and health-related factors (European Union, 2013). The 1978 reform also introduced a decentralized governance structure, with the regions assuming responsibility for the organization and delivery of healthcare services within their territories (Giorgi, 2023). This decentralization was further reinforced by subsequent reforms in the 1990s (Legislative Decrees 502/1992 and 517/1993), which granted the regions even greater autonomy in healthcare planning, financing, and management.

The early 1990s saw the introduction of managerial principles into the SSN, with the aim of improving efficiency and accountability and ensuring that all citizens receive essential levels of care. Local health units (Unità Sanitarie Locali, USL) were transformed into local health enterprises (Aziende Sanitarie Locali, ASL), and larger hospitals were given greater autonomy as hospital/healthcare organizations (Aziende Ospedaliere, AO). A diagnosis-related group (DRG) prospective payment system for hospital care and a fee-for-service system for outpatient care were also introduced during this period (Bosa et al., 2021).

The decentralization process of the 1990s had a significant impact on the functioning of the SSN (France & Taroni, 2005). On the one hand, it allowed for greater flexibility and responsiveness to local needs, as regions and health authorities were able to tailor their services to the specific characteristics of their populations. On the other hand, it also led to a greater variability in the quality and accessibility of healthcare services across the country, with some regions (particularly in the south) struggling to ensure adequate levels of care (Bosa et al., 2021).

In the late 1990s and early 2000s, concerns about rising healthcare expenditures and regional disparities in access to care and health outcomes led to further reforms. The National Health Plan for 1998–2000 sought to reaffirm the role of the central government in ensuring essential levels of care (Livelli Essenziali di Assistenza, LEA) across the country (Torbica & Fattore, 2005). The LEA were defined as a set of health services that the SSN was required to provide uniformly across all regions, regardless of their economic or organizational capacity (Ministero della Salute, 2019b). In 1999, the latest major health reform, Law 229/1999 also known as the "Bindi decree" or the Third Reform, completed the necessary process of organization and rationalization to achieve an efficient and effective national health service (Parlamento Italiano, 1999).

The 2001 constitutional reform (Title V) further strengthened the role of the regions in healthcare policy but also introduced the concept of fiscal federalism, requiring the regions to cover any deficits incurred in the provision of LEA (Bosa et al., 2021). This reform marked a significant shift in the financing of the SSN, as regions were now required to raise their own resources (through regional taxes and co-payments) to fund healthcare services, in addition to the funds received from the central government. Since this constitutional reform, public healthcare in Italy has been shaped using agreements between state and regions as a main tool.

The introduction of fiscal federalism had important implications for the equity and sustainability of the SSN (Rotulo et al., 2020). While some regions (particularly in the north) were able to successfully manage their healthcare budgets and ensure high levels of care, others (mostly in the south) struggled to generate sufficient resources and maintain adequate services (Liberati, 2003). This led to growing regional disparities in access to care and health outcomes, with some areas of the country experiencing significant gaps in the provision of essential services (European Commission, 2023a; Fina et al., 2021; Matranga & Maniscalco, 2022).

The economic crisis of the late 2000s and early 2010s had a significant impact on the Italian healthcare system, leading to cost-containment measures and austerity policies (Ferré et al., 2018; Neri, 2019). Several regions, mostly in the south, were unable to meet their fiscal obligations and were required to implement recovery plans (Piani di Rientro) under the supervision of the central government. The mechanism of recovery plans began to be used in 2007, even before the crisis, and within 3 years, it involved ten regions, seven of which were still under recovery plans in 2020. These recovery plans often involved cuts to healthcare spending, reorganization of services, and measures to improve efficiency and appropriateness of care

(Bordignon et al., 2020; Depalo, 2019). It is evident that being subjected to the recovery plan mechanism, which has a certain financial effectiveness, has significantly reduced the autonomy of the affected regions (Neri, 2020).

The control measures implemented in response to the economic crisis had a significant impact on the functioning and accessibility of the SSN (Chisari & Lega, 2023). They have affected all areas, from personnel to pharmaceutical spending and purchases of goods and services, to hospital beds, and to investment spending (Neri, 2020).

Between 2010 and 2019, public health expenditure in Italy was approximately zero (+0.1%) in real terms, while per capita expenditure growth was about +10.8% (World Bank Group, 2024), which led to an increased gap between Italy's public health expenditure and that of other countries, like France and Germany, which is higher (OECD, 2020). This gap has been only partially mitigated by an increase in private spending. In fact, out-of-pocket payments increased by 9.5% (OECD, 2019).

Even if there have been no legislative changes from the constitutional reform of 2001, these processes have significantly weakened the role of the regions in national policymaking. As a result, this picture has enhanced the role of the central government, the Ministry of the Economy and Finance, and the European institutions (Neri, 2020).

Despite these challenges, the SSN has demonstrated a remarkable resilience and capacity to adapt to changing circumstances (Parotto et al., 2023). In recent years, there has been a growing emphasis on the integration of health and social care services, the development of community-based care models, and the promotion of prevention and healthy lifestyles. The SSN has also been at the forefront of important public health initiatives, such as the introduction of compulsory vaccinations for children and the implementation of comprehensive tobacco control policies (European Commission, 2023a).

The COVID-19 pandemic has further tested the resilience of the SSN and highlighted both its strengths and weaknesses (Armocida et al., 2020; Genova & Lombardini, 2024; Neri, 2020). On the one hand, the system has demonstrated a remarkable capacity to mobilize resources and coordinate efforts in response to the crisis, with health professionals and institutions working nonstop to provide care and support to affected populations. On the other hand, the pandemic has also exposed long-standing structural weaknesses, such as the fragmentation of primary care services, the lack of investment in public health infrastructures, and the persistent regional disparities in access to care (Cicchetti et al., 2021; Odone et al., 2020; Parotto et al., 2023).

Thus, the existing tensions in the Italian SSN became evident with the onset of the COVID pandemic (Neri, 2020). The government was forced to exercise its powers not only by dialoguing with the regions but also proceeding unilaterally due to the urgency of the situation that called for quick decision-making and measures. To some extent, this represents a continuation of the trend towards centralized decision-making and regulation from previous years, intensified "in wartime" during the coronavirus crisis (Neri, 2020).

The regions have faced an extremely difficult and new situation, finding themselves on the front lines as the authorities responsible for health services (Ricci et al., 2020). However, many have managed to seize the emergency as an opportunity to affirm their relevance in the institutional system and, even more, their importance to citizens. While previous years were marked by a crisis of the regional entity, the pandemic has quite paradoxically provided a chance for the regions to regain their legitimacy (Neri, 2020).

The strengthening of regional institutional identity has also been supported by the differences in responses among regions, whether hospital-centered or community-based (Bosa et al., 2021; Romiti et al., 2023). Regardless of their effectiveness, this diversity highlighted the existence and importance of regional health models, which had been partially obscured by a trend towards similar organizational solutions in previous years driven by the need to rationalize and contain health expenditure (Neri, 2019). The pandemic has shown that regional models exist and matter, making effective regional governance and administration as important as competent local or central institutions and leaders (Fig. 3.1).

Looking ahead, the Italian National Health Service faces a number of important challenges and opportunities (Neri, 2020). The aging of the population, the rising burden of chronic diseases, and the increasing costs of medical technologies will require a sustained effort to ensure the long-term sustainability and effectiveness of the system (OECD, 2023). At the same time, the SSN has the potential to leverage

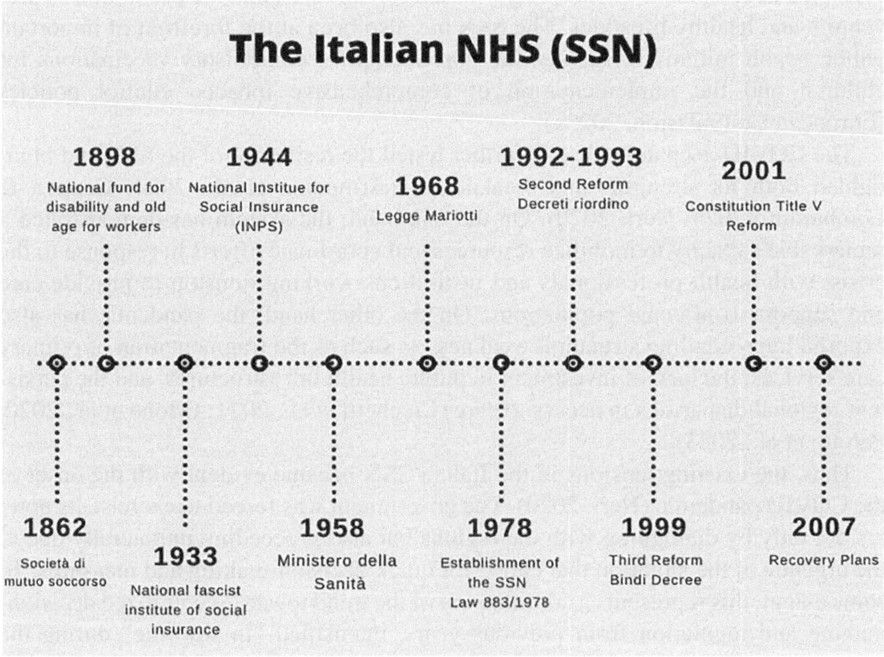

Fig. 3.1 Italian SSN timeline. *Source*: own elaboration

new technologies, such as telemedicine and personalized medicine, to improve the quality and accessibility of care, particularly for underserved populations and remote areas (Cingolani et al., 2023; OECD, 2023; Tarricone et al., 2021).

To meet these challenges and seize these opportunities, the SSN will need to continue to evolve and adapt, building on its core values of universalism, solidarity, and equity while also embracing innovation and change (Tanese, 2023). This will require an effort by all stakeholders—policymakers, health professionals, patients, and patients' organizations—to work together to develop a more responsive, efficient, and sustainable healthcare system.

3.2.2 Principles and Organization of the Italian National Healthcare System

The SSN is founded on a set of core principles that guide its organization and functioning. These principles are included in the Italian Constitution (Article 32) and expressed in the law establishing the SSN (Law 833/1978). They reflect the fundamental values of the Italian welfare state and the commitment to ensuring the right to health for all citizens.

The first and most important principle is that of universality, which establishes that all individuals have the right to access essential healthcare services, regardless of their social, economic, or legal status. This principle is based on the recognition that health is a fundamental human right and that the state has a responsibility to ensure that this right is upheld for all its citizens (Legge 833/1978).

The second principle is that of solidarity, which emphasizes the collective responsibility of society to support and care for its most vulnerable members (Legge 833/1978). In other words, this means that the system is financed through taxation, with resources pooled and allocated according to need, rather than by ability to pay. This ensures that the financial burden of healthcare is shared equitably across society and that no individual is left without access to essential services due to financial constraints.

The third principle is that of equity, which requires that healthcare services be distributed fairly and according to need, rather than other factors such as income, social status, or geographic location (Legge 833/1978). This principle is reflected in the establishment of the essential levels of care (LEA), which—as previously introduced—define a set of health services that must be guaranteed to all citizens, regardless of where they live or their individual circumstances (Ministero della Salute, 2019b).

LEA are a crucial component of the SSN, as they establish a common baseline of services that all regions and health authorities are required to provide (Ministero della Salute, 2019b). LEA cover a wide range of preventive, diagnostic, therapeutic, and rehabilitative services, including hospital care, outpatient specialist care, pharmaceuticals, and medical devices (Torbica & Fattore, 2005). The specific services

Table 3.1 Core principles of the Italian SSN. *Source*: own elaboration

Principle	Description	Key elements
Universality	All individuals have the right to access essential health care services, regardless of social, economic, or legal status.	• Health as a fundamental human right • State's responsibility to uphold this right
Solidarity	Emphasizes collective responsibility to support and care for the most vulnerable members of society.	• Financed through taxation • Resources pooled and allocated by need • Equitable financial burden sharing
Equity	Health care services must be distributed fairly and according to need, not factors like income, social status, or geographic location.	• Establishment of essential levels of care (LEA) • Guaranteed set of health services for all citizens

included in the LEA are determined by the Ministry of Health, based on scientific evidence and public health priorities, and are subject to periodic revision and update (Donatini, 2015; Table 3.1).

To ensure that the LEA are effectively implemented across the country, the SSN relies on a system of monitoring and evaluation, conducted by the National Agency for Regional Health Services (Agenzia Nazionale per i Servizi Sanitari Regionali, AGENAS). AGENAS is responsible for assessing the performance of regional health systems in delivering the LEA, using a set of indicators that measure the quality, appropriateness, and efficiency of care (Ministero della Salute, 2019a; Ministero della Salute, 2021). There are still too many disparities across Italian regions as not all of them grant LEA to their citizens (Bartoloni, 2024). Regions that fail to meet the LEA standards may be subject to financial penalties and required to implement corrective measures.

The organization of the SSN at the regional level is based on a model of decentralization and autonomy, with each region having the authority to plan, organize, and manage its own health services, within the framework of the national guidelines and standards (Donatini, 2020). This model allows for a degree of flexibility and responsiveness to local needs and preferences but also requires a strong system of coordination and cooperation between the different levels of government and the various actors involved in the healthcare system (France et al., 2005).

One of the key challenges in the organization of the SSN is to ensure an appropriate balance between the need for national-level coordination and standardization, on the one hand, and the need for regional and local autonomy and flexibility, on the other (Ricciardi & Tarricone, 2021). This requires a constant process of negotiation and adaptation, as well as the development of effective mechanisms for shared decision-making, performance monitoring, and accountability (Bruzzi et al., 2022).

Another important challenge is to ensure the effective integration and continuity of care across the different levels and settings of the healthcare system (Ferré et al.,

2014). This requires the development of strong primary care services, capable of providing comprehensive and coordinated care to patients over time, as well as the establishment of effective referral and communication systems between primary care providers, specialists, and hospitals (i.e., Nuti et al., 2020).

In recent years, there has been a growing emphasis on the development of integrated care models, which seek to promote greater collaboration and coordination between health and social care services, particularly for patients with complex and chronic conditions (Cinelli & Fattore, 2024; Ferrara et al., 2022). These models often involve the establishment of multidisciplinary teams (Tousijn, 2012), the use of case management and care planning tools, and the deployment of information and communication technologies to support the sharing of information and the coordination of care (European Commission, 2023b).

Therefore, the organization of the Italian National Health Service reflects a complex interplay of national, regional, and local actors and institutions, each with their own roles, responsibilities, and interests (i.e., Romiti et al., 2023). While this decentralized structure presents challenges in terms of coordination and standardization, it also allows for a degree of flexibility and responsiveness to the diverse needs and preferences of the Italian population. As the SSN continues to evolve and adapt to new challenges and opportunities, it will be important to maintain a focus on the core principles of universality, solidarity, and equity while also fostering innovation and experimentation in the organization and delivery of care (Cicchetti et al., 2021).

3.2.3 Healthcare Institutions in Italy

The Italian healthcare system comprises a wide range of healthcare institutions, each playing a specific role in the delivery of healthcare services and the promotion of public health. These organizations operate within the framework of the SSN, collaborating and coordinating their activities to ensure the provision of comprehensive and high-quality care to the population (Table 3.2).

At the national level, the Ministry of Health is the main governing body of the SSN. It is responsible for national health planning, defining essential levels of care (LEA), allocating financial resources to regions, and coordinating healthcare policies and programs (Ministero della Salute, 2024a). The National Institute of Health (Istituto Superiore di Sanità, ISS) is the primary technical-scientific body of the SSN. It conducts research, provides technical and scientific advice to the Ministry of Health and other institutions, and supports in the development of guidelines and standards for healthcare services (Ministero della Salute, 2024a). The Italian Medicines Agency (Agenzia Italiana del Farmaco (AIFA)) is responsible for the regulation and supervision of pharmaceuticals. Moreover, the National Agency for Regional Healthcare Services (Agenzia Nazionale per i Servizi Sanitari Regionali (AGENAS)) supports regions in the planning, organization, and evaluation of healthcare services. It promotes the dissemination of best practices and the development of performance measurement systems (Ministero della Salute, 2024a).

Table 3.2 Key institutions in the Italian healthcare system. *Source*: own elaboration

Institution	Role	Key responsibilities
Ministry of Health	Main governing body of the SSN	• National health planning • Defining essential levels of care (LEA) • Allocating financial resources to regions • Coordinating healthcare policies
National Agency for Regional Health Services (AGENAS)	Monitoring and evaluation of regional health systems in delivering LEA.	• Assessing performance using quality, appropriateness, and efficiency indicators. • Imposing financial penalties and corrective measures for non-compliance.
National Institute of Health (ISS)	Conducting scientific research and providing technical support on public health issues.	• Scientific research • Technical support • Public health issue guidance
Italian Medicines Agency (AIFA)	Regulation and supervision of pharmaceuticals.	• Pharmaceutical regulation • Supervision of medicine safety and effectiveness
Local Health Authorities (ASL)	Delivery of primary care, preventive services, and outpatient specialist care at the regional level.	• Primary care delivery • Preventive services • Outpatient specialist care
Hospital Organizations (AO)	Providing inpatient hospital care and complex diagnostic and therapeutic procedures.	• Inpatient hospital care • Complex diagnostic and therapeutic procedures
University Hospital (AOU)	Ensuring provision of hospital care, established by regional authorities after an experimental phase introduced by Legislative Decree 517/1999.	• Provision of hospital care • Implementation varied by regional healthcare contexts
Scientific Institutes for Research, Hospitalization, and Healthcare (IRCCS)	Combining healthcare provision with biomedical research	• Conducting basic, translational, and clinical research • Collaborating with universities and research institutions • Training healthcare professionals

At the regional level, the SSN is organized around a network of local health authorities (ASL) and hospital/healthcare organizations (AO). ASLs are responsible for the delivery of primary care, preventive services, and outpatient specialist care, while AOs provide inpatient hospital care and more complex diagnostic and therapeutic procedures. The Legislative Decree 517/1999 introduced an additional entity in the landscape of those responsible for ensuring the provision of hospital care, the University Hospitals (Aziende Ospedaliero-Universitarie). These are to be established by the various regional authorities after a maximum 4-year experimental phase. The experience gained during the implementation phase of this Legislative Decree (517/1999) revealed a varied picture of the outcomes of this experimental phase, depending on the regional healthcare contexts (D'Alema et al., 2010).

A unique feature of the Italian healthcare system is the presence of Scientific Institutes for Research, Hospitalization, and Healthcare (Istituti di Ricovero e Cura a Carattere Scientifico, IRCCS). These institutes combine healthcare provision with biomedical research, focusing on specific disease areas or disciplines (Ministero della Salute, 2022). The Ministry of Health recognizes IRCCS for their scientific excellence and ability to translate research findings into clinical practice. They receive public funding to support research activities and are subject to periodic evaluation to maintain their status. IRCCS play a crucial role in advancing biomedical research and innovation in Italy by conducting basic, translational, and clinical research, often in collaboration with universities, research institutions, and industry partners (Ministero della Salute, 2024a). They also contribute to training healthcare professionals and disseminating scientific knowledge (Ministero della Salute, 2024a).

3.2.4 IRCCS: A Closer Look

The Scientific Institutes for Research, Hospitalization, and Healthcare (IRCCS) are a vital component of the Italian healthcare system. These institutes combine excellence in healthcare provision with cutting-edge research, focusing on specific disease areas or disciplines (Ministero della Salute, 2024a, b).

Historical Evolution and Legal Framework

IRCCS first appeared in a Royal Decree in 1938, "General norms for the organization of hospital services and personnel," which distinguished them from other hospitals because, in addition to hospitalization and patient care, they also conducted scientific research to improve healthcare through the application of basic research discoveries (Gazzella Ufficiale, 2022).

In the first 15 years following the Royal Decree, only three hospitals were recognized as IRCCS: the Regina Elena Institute in Rome, the National Institute for the Study and Treatment of Tumors in Milan, and the Pascale Foundation in Naples, all focused on cancer research and treatment (Gazzella Ufficiale, 2022). The Second World War stopped the establishment of new IRCCS until the 1950s, when the Besta Institute in Milan, nervous system diseases, and the Gaslini Institute in Genoa, maternal and child healthcare, were recognized (Gazzella Ufficiale, 2022).

As of 2024, the Italian healthcare system counts 54 IRCCS, comprising 24 public and 30 private institutes (Ministero della Salute, 2024a). These are strategically distributed across the country, aiming to ensure a comprehensive coverage of various clinical and research areas. The most well-represented field is oncology, with 13 dedicated institutes focusing on the study and treatment of cancer (Gazzella Ufficiale, 2022). This highlights the significant burden of cancer on the Italian population and the nation's commitment to advancing oncological research and care.

Among the list of IRCCS, there are five institutes specializing in complex medicine, addressing the challenges posed by multifaceted and chronic conditions that require a multidisciplinary approach (Gazzella Ufficiale, 2022). Infectious diseases, a field that has gained renewed prominence in the wake of the COVID-19 pandemic, are covered by two institutes. Additionally, there are institutes dedicated to diagnostic imaging, neurology, neurorehabilitation, psychiatry, rehabilitation, gastroenterology, cardiology, dermatology, pediatrics, orthopedics, genetics, geriatrics, pharmacology, ophthalmology, and personalized medicine and innovative biotechnologies (Gazzella Ufficiale, 2022; Ministero della Salute, 2024b; Tables 3.3 and 3.4).

Table 3.3 List of public IRCCS and areas of expertise. *Source*: adapted from Ministero della Salute (2024b)

Healthcare Organization	Research Area	Decree	State (as of June 2024)
Istituto Oncologico Veneto - Padova	Oncology	Decreto 4 agosto 2023	Confirmed
Ospedale infantile Burlo Garofolo - Trieste	Maternal and child health	Decreto 26 gennaio 2024	Confirmed
CRO - Centro di Riferimento Oncologico - Aviano (PN)	Oncology	Decreto 30 ottobre 2020	Confirmed
Fondazione IRCCS San Gerardo dei Tintori - Monza (MB)	Pediatrics	Decreto 12 ottobre 2022	Approved
Fondazione Istituto Neurologico Carlo Besta - Milano	Diseases of nervous system in adults and children	Decreto 20 gennaio 2021	Confirmed
Fondazione IRCCS Istituto Nazionale dei tumori - Milano	Oncology	Decreto 15 luglio 2020	Confirmed
Fondazione Ca'Granda – Ospedale Maggiore Policlinico - Milano	Repair and replacement of cells, organs, and tissues	Decreto 4 dicembre 2020	Confirmed
Fondazione Policlinico San Matteo - Pavia	Emergency-urgency in adults and children Transplant: disease treatable with organ, tissue, and cell transplant Internal medicine diseases with high biomedical and technological complexity	Decreto 21 gennaio 2021	Confirmed
Istituto delle Scienze Neurologiche - Bologna	Neurological sciences	Decreto 3 luglio 2023	Confirmed
Istituto Ortopedico Rizzoli - Bologna	Orthopedics and traumatology	Decreto 2 novembre 2020	Confirmed
Azienda Ospedaliero Universitaria - Bologna	Transplant assistance and research in clinical patients Integrated medical and surgical management of oncological diseases	Decreto 19 settembre 2020 Decreto di rettifica 23 aprile 2021	Approved
Istituto in tecnologie avanzate e modelli assistenziali in oncologia - Reggio Emilia	Oncology for advanced technologies and care models	Decreto 16 luglio 2020	Confirmed
Istituto Giannina Gaslini - Genova	Maternal and child health	Decreto 17 novembre 2021	Confirmed
Ospedale Policlinico San Martino - Genova	Oncology Neurological sciences	Decreto 3 maggio 2021	Confirmed
Istituto Nazionale di Riposo e Cura per Anziani - Ancona	Geriatrics	Decreto 1 agosto 2023	Confirmed
Azienda ospedaliero-universitaria Meyer - Firenze	Pediatrics	Decreto 2 agosto 2022	Approved
Istituti fisioterapici ospitalieri - Istituto Regina Elena Istituti fisioterapici ospitalieri - Istituto Dermatologico Santa Maria e San Gallicano - Roma	Oncology Dermatology	Decreto 8 maggio 2020	Confirmed
Istituto per le Malattie Infettive Lazzaro Spallanzani - Roma	Infectious diseases	Decreto 7 agosto 2023	Confirmed
Istituto nazionale tumori Fondazione Giovanni Pascale - Napoli	Oncology	Decreto 16 maggio 2022	Confirmed
Ente Ospedaliero specializzato in gastroenterologia Saverio De Bellis - Castellana Grotte (BA)	Gastroenterology	Decreto 10 novembre 2021	Confirmed
Istituto tumori Giovanni Paolo II - Bari	Oncology	Decreto 8 marzo 2023	Confirmed
CROB Centro di riferimento oncologico della Basilicata- Rionero in Vulture (PZ)	Oncology	Decreto 9 giugno 2022	Confirmed
IRCCS Centro Neurolesi Bonino Pulejo- Messina	Neurosciences in the field of prevention, recovery, and treatment of severe acquired neurological injuries	Decreto 23 novembre 2021	Confirmed

This diverse range of specialties reflects the commitment of the Italian healthcare system to address the varied health needs of the population, from the most prevalent conditions to rare and complex diseases. The current distribution of IRCCS in Italy reflects a strategic approach to healthcare planning, aiming to allocate resources and expertise where they are most needed. By concentrating highly specialized care and research in specific centers of excellence, the Italian healthcare system can optimize the use of resources, foster collaboration among experts, and ultimately improve patient outcomes (Ministero della Salute, 2019a, b).

The process of recognizing an institution as an IRCCS is rigorous and selective, involving a thorough evaluation by the Ministry of Health in collaboration with the President of the interested region (Ministero della Salute, 2024a). This evaluation assesses the institute's scientific excellence, research output, and ability to translate research findings into clinical practice (Gazzella Ufficiale, 2022).

Table 3.4 List of private IRCCS and areas of expertise. *Source*: adapted from Ministero della Salute (2024b)

Healthcare Organization	Research Area	Decree	State (as of June 2024)
San Camillo IRCCS S.r.l. - Venezia	Motor, communication, and behavioral neurorehabilitation	Decreto 26 gennaio 2024	Confirmed
IRCCS Centro San Giovanni di Dio Fatebenefratelli - Brescia	Psychiatric diseases	Decreto 23 dicembre 2021	Confirmed
Centro Cardiologico S.P.A. Fondazione Monzino - Milano	Cardiovascular diseases	Decreto 24 gennaio 2022	Confirmed
IEO - Istituto Europeo di Oncologia - Milano	Oncological diseases	Decreto 15 settembre 2021	Confirmed
Istituto Ortopedico Galeazzi - Milano	Musculoskeletal diseases	Decreto 22 marzo 2021	Confirmed
Istituto Auxologico Italiano - Milano	Cardiology-pulmonology, endocrinology, and neurology	Decreto 26 gennaio 2024	Confirmed
IRCCS Ospedale San Raffaele - Milano	Molecular medicine	Decreto 3 luglio 2023	Confirmed
IRCCS Multimedica - Milano	Cardiovascular diseases	Decreto 26 aprile 2023	Confirmed
Fondazione Don Carlo Gnocchi - Milano	Rehabilitation medicine	Decreto 26 gennaio 2024	Confirmed
Istituto di ricerche farmacologiche Mario Negri - Milano, Bergamo, Ranica	Pharmacology and clinical trials on neurological, rare, and environmental diseases	Decreto 3 maggio 2021	Confirmed
Istituto Clinico Humanitas - Rozzano (Milano)	Immunodegenerative diseases	Decreto 25 settembre 2023	Confirmed
Policlinico San Donato - San Donato Milanese	Diseases of the heart and major vessels in adults and children	Decreto 26 settembre 2023	Confirmed
Fondazione Istituto Neurologico Casimiro Mondino - Pavia	Nervous system diseases	Decreto 9 giugno 2022	Confirmed
Istituti Clinici Scientifici Maugeri S.p.A. SB - Pavia	Rehabilitation	Decreto 26 gennaio 2024	Confirmed
Istituto Eugenio Medea - Bosisio Parini (LC)	Rehabilitation medicine	Decreto 10 luglio 2023	Confirmed
Fondazione del Piemonte per l'Oncologia - Candiolo (TO)	Oncology	Decreto 7 aprile 2022	Confirmed
Ospedale Sacro Cuore Don Calabria- Negrar (VR)	Infectious and tropical diseases	Decreto 27 luglio 2021	Confirmed
Istituto scientifico romagnolo per lo studio e la cura dei tumori- Meldola (FC)	Advanced therapies in medical oncology	Decreto 9 agosto 2021	Confirmed
Fondazione Stella Maris - Calambrone (Pisa)	Child and adolescent neuropsychiatry	Decreto 26 gennaio 2024	Confirmed
Fondazione G.B. Bietti per lo studio e la ricerca in oftalmologia - Roma	Ophthalmology	Decreto 5 luglio 2022	Confirmed
Fondazione Policlinico Universitario Agostino Gemelli - Roma	Personalized medicine Innovative biotechnologies	Decreto 10 novembre 2021	Approved
Fondazione Santa Lucia - Roma	Neuromotor rehabilitation with extension to the field of neurosciences	Decreto 19 luglio 2022	Confirmed
Ospedale pediatrico Bambino Gesù - Roma	Pediatrics	Decreto 30 ottobre 2023	Confirmed
Istituto Dermopatico dell'Immacolata (IDI)- Roma	Dermatology	Decreto 9 luglio 2019	Confirmed
IRCCS San Raffaele Pisana- Roma	Motor and sensory rehabilitation	Decreto 10 novembre 2020	Confirmed
Istituto Neurologico Mediterraneo Neuromed - Pozzilli (IS)	Neurosciences	Decreto 9 agosto 2021	Confirmed
SYNLAB SDN - Napoli	Integrated imaging and laboratory diagnostics	Decreto 8 marzo 2023	Confirmed
Ospedale Casa Sollievo della Sofferenza - San Giovanni Rotondo (FG)	Genetic diseases, innovative therapies, and regenerative medicine	Decreto 17 aprile 2020	Confirmed
Istituto Mediterraneo per i Trapianti e Terapie ad Alta Specializzazione (ISMETT) - Palermo	Care and research of terminal organ insufficiencies	Decreto 1 ottobre 2019	Confirmed
Oasi di Maria Santissima - Troina (EN)	Mental retardation and senile cerebral involution	Decreto 22 novembre 2018	Confirmed

There are stringent criteria for IRCCS recognition with the aim of guaranteeing that only institutions with a proven track record of outstanding performance in both research and patient care are granted this prestigious status (Ministero della Salute, 2024a). The IRCCS status is reviewed every 2 years to ensure that they continue to meet the standards of excellence specifics of these institutions (Gazzella Ufficiale, 2022). Each year, their research and service activities and outputs are evaluated to determine the distribution of the ministerial funds (Gazzella Ufficiale, 2022).

The allocation of current research funds is based on five main criteria, each having a different weight (Ministero della Salute, 2023): First, the criterion concerning the clinical activity, which accounts for 20% of the total evaluation. It measures several aspects of patient care. For example, it includes the number of hospital admissions for the five most frequent diagnosis-related groups relevant to the area of recognition of the IRCCS, the complexity of the case treated, and the efficiency and effectiveness of the care provided (Gazzella Ufficiale, 2022). Importantly, this criterion also includes the ability to attract both national and international patients (Gazzella Ufficiale, 2022; Ministero della Salute, 2023).

Second, the criterion concerning the scientific production is the most heavily weighted (55%). It evaluates the impact factor of publications, the number and ranking authors in scientific publications, and the overall impact of scientific activity. It also includes the cost-effectiveness of scientific outputs, taking into account the average productivity, performance, and publications (Gazzella Ufficiale, 2022; Ministero della Salute, 2023).

The third criterion is the capacity to operate in a network, which holds a 10% weight (Gazzella Ufficiale, 2022). It focuses on the extent at which the IRCCS is capable of engaging in multicenter programs. To assess this criterion, the variables that are looked upon are, for instance, the number of patients per year enrolled in multicentric programs, the number of multicentric clinical trials in which a researcher from the IRCCS act as the primary investigator, as well as the number of trials in which the institution is an active participant (Ministero della Salute, 2023).

The fourth criterion concerns the capacity to attract resources, which also holds a percent of 10 on the overall evaluation (Gazzella Ufficiale, 2022). Through this criterion, the Italian Ministry of Health aims at evaluating the total funding obtained from both public and private entities, being either from national or international funds (Ministero della Salute, 2023). The fifth and last criterion considered is the technology transfer which, for now, only accounts for the 5% of the total evaluation (Gazzella Ufficiale, 2022). It aims at considering the economic values of the patents licensed by the IRCCS, and it considers the past 3 years, as well as those in which the patent is co-signed by the IRCCS (Ministero della Salute, 2023).

However, the concentration of IRCCS in certain regions, particularly in the north of Italy, has also raised concerns about potential disparities in access to advanced care and research opportunities. Efforts have been made to address this issue by promoting collaboration and knowledge-sharing among IRCCS across different regions, as well as by investing in the development of new IRCCS in underserved areas.

The Role of Collaboration and Integration Among IRCCS

The integration of research, healthcare, and training is a fundamental principle that characterizes IRCCS (Ministero della Salute, 2019a, b). These institutes play a crucial role in the national healthcare system, as they combine high-quality diagnostic and therapeutic activities with excellent biomedical research (Gazzella Ufficiale, 2022; Ministero della Salute, 2019a, b, 2024a).

One of the distinctive features of IRCCS is the opportunity, strongly encouraged by the Ministry of Health, of engaging in collaboration among the various structures (Garattini et al., 2022; Ministero della Salute, 2023). This allows for the optimization of resources, sharing of knowledge and expertise, and coordinated work on ambitious multicenter projects. Collaborations among IRCCS enable them to be more competitive internationally and to more rapidly translate research findings into patient care (Ministero della Salute, 2023).

There are many examples of these collaborations, one of which is represented by the thematic networks of IRCCS (Garattini et al., 2022). There are several operational networks, such as, among others, the oncology network, the neuroscience and neurorehabilitation network, and the cardiology network. These networks bring together IRCCS working on common thematic areas, allowing them to share protocols, databases, equipment, and specific skills (Garattini et al., 2022). This gives the chances to strongly enhance the research capabilities of the entire healthcare system (Table 3.5).

Another example of the close integration among IRCCS is the development of shared technological platforms, such as in the case of the neuroscience and neurorehabilitation network, which is implementing common platforms for neuroimaging, genomics, and tele-rehabilitation (Gazzella Ufficiale, 2022). Again, sharing resources and know-how significantly amplifies the potential of the individual institute.

The thematic networks have also created "Virtual National Institutes" dedicated to specific diseases (e.g., dementias, rare diseases, multiple sclerosis), where researchers and clinicians from various IRCCS work together on common projects using multidisciplinary approaches (Gazzella Ufficiale, 2022). This allows for the creation of critical mass on issues of great relevance to public health. Moreover, IRCCS are actively involved in training the next generation of healthcare professionals and researchers. The close integration of research, care, and education within these institutes provides a unique environment for hands-on learning and the rapid translation of research findings into clinical practice (Gazzella Ufficiale, 2022; Ministero della Salute, 2023; Ministero della Salute, 2024a, b). Many IRCCS have strong ties with universities and offer residency programs, PhD courses, and other educational opportunities (Bachelet, 2008).

Table 3.5 Overview of established IRCCS thematic networks. *Source*: Lodi (2023)

IRCCS Network Name	Year of Establishment	Number of participating IRCCS
Alliance Against Cancer (ACC)	2002	27
Cardiology Network (CARDIO)	2017	20
Neuroscience and Neurorehabilitation Network (RIN)	2017	30
Italian Network for Health in Developmental Age (Rete IDEA)	2017	11
Aging Network	2017	13
Musculoskeletal System Network (RAMS)	2019	7

The IRCCS are also at the forefront of implementing precision medicine approaches. The close collaboration among clinicians, researchers, and technology experts within and across institutes allows for the development of personalized diagnostic and therapeutic strategies based on the individual characteristics of each patient (Gazzella Ufficiale, 2022). The sharing of data and biological samples among IRCCS, facilitated by the thematic networks, is fundamental in developing large patient cohorts and "biobanks" for advancing precision medicine.

Therefore, the integration of research, care, and training that characterizes the IRCCS finds its highest expression in the ability to "work as a system" to be competitive and innovative at an international level (Bachelet, 2008). The IRCCS model, based on close collaboration and sharing of resources and expertise, represents an example of excellence in the biomedical field and should be considered as a strategic asset for the Italian healthcare system.

Research Funding and Scientific Output

IRCCS play a pivotal role in advancing biomedical research in Italy, and their scientific output is a proof of the significant investment in research funding from both public and private sources (Ministero della Salute, 2024a, b). The Ministry of Health is a key supporter of IRCCS research activities, providing dedicated funding through a competitive process that takes into account the institutes' scientific production and the quality of their research projects. In 2022, the Ministry of Health allocated a total of €218 million to fund IRCCS research, highlighting the government's commitment to supporting scientific excellence in the healthcare sector (Lodi, 2023).

In addition to the funding provided by the Ministry of Health, IRCCS benefit from a diverse range of research grants from other public and private entities. The European Union, for example, is a significant source of funding for collaborative research projects involving IRCCS and other European institutions. The Italian Ministry of Education, Universities and Research (MIUR) also provides support for basic and translational research conducted at IRCCS. Private foundations and industry partners are increasingly recognizing the value of investing in IRCCS research, as evidenced by the substantial contributions received from these sources (Gazzella Ufficiale, 2022).

The scientific output of IRCCS is remarkable, both in terms of quantity and quality. On average, IRCCS produce approximately 12,000 scientific publications annually, covering a wide range of research topics and disciplines (Gazzella Ufficiale, 2022). These manuscripts are published in top-tier national and international journals (Ministero della Salute, 2022), which highlights the global impact and visibility of IRCCS' research. This reflects also on the country, to be recognized as an important incubator of research, innovation, and patient care. The total normalized impact factor of IRCCS publications, a measure of the scientific influence and citation impact of research, is over the 50,000 points, further underlining the significance of their scientific contributions (Ministero della Salute, 2022).

Table 3.6 Key statistics of IRCCS (2022). *Source*: adapted from Lodi (2023) and Guglielmi (2023). *Data related to the specific areas of expertise of IRCCS. **Of which 11,911 with at least 1 publication

IRCCS N° Researchers	13,952**
IRCCS - N° scientific publications (*)	18,852
IRCCS - Total Normalized Impact Factor (*)	102,783
IRCCS - N° annual hospitalizations	692,596
Acute	*632,899*
Rehabilitation	*41,922*
Long-term care and Others	*17,775*

In addition to their research activities, IRCCS play a crucial role in providing highly specialized healthcare services. The 54 IRCCS collectively perform around 700,000 hospitalizations per year (Guglielmi, 2023), offering advanced diagnostic, therapeutic, and rehabilitative interventions to patients with complex and rare conditions. This unique combination of research excellence and clinical expertise positions IRCCS as key drivers of innovation in the Italian healthcare system, enabling the rapid translation of scientific research and discoveries into improved patient care (Table 3.6).

IRCCS are increasingly pushed towards competitive grant schemes and public-private partnerships. They are, in fact, encouraged to diversify their funding sources and collaborate with national and international partners to secure the resources needed to sustain and expand their research activities.

Still, challenges remain in ensuring an equitable distribution of research funding across different regions and disciplines. There is a need for a more balanced allocation of resources, taking into account the specific needs and priorities of each region and the potential impact of research on public health (Lodi, 2023). Efforts are being made to strengthen the coordination and harmonization of research funding mechanisms at the national level, promoting a more strategic and coherent approach to research investment in the healthcare sector (Lodi, 2023).

Future Perspectives and Recent Reform

The IRCCS system is continuously evolving to adapt to the changing healthcare and research landscape, with a strong focus on excellence, innovation, and patient-centered care (Ministero della Salute, 2022, 2024a). The recent reform introduced by Legislative Decree 200/2022 aims to further strengthen the role of IRCCS as key players in the national and international research landscape while promoting their integration with other components of the healthcare system (Gazzella Ufficiale, 2022).

One of the primary objectives of the reform is to enhance the translational nature of IRCCS research, ensuring that scientific findings are rapidly and effectively translated into clinical practice and patient care. This involves fostering closer collaboration between researchers, streamlining the process of technology transfer, and promoting the adoption of innovative diagnostic and therapeutic approaches (Gazzella Ufficiale, 2022).

To achieve this goal, the reform emphasizes the importance of personalized medicine, recognizing the potential of tailored interventions based on an individual's genetic, environmental, and lifestyle factors. IRCCS are encouraged to develop closer partnerships with universities and industry partners to advance the development of personalized therapies, biomarkers, and diagnostic tools (Gazzella Ufficiale, 2022). This collaborative approach is expected to accelerate the translation of scientific discoveries into tangible benefits for patients while also promoting economic growth and competitiveness in the biomedical sector (Guglielmi, 2023).

The reform also highlights the critical role of IRCCS in driving the digital transformation of healthcare. As the healthcare system becomes increasingly data-driven, IRCCS are expected to leverage their expertise in data science, artificial intelligence, and telemedicine to develop new tools and approaches for the diagnosis, treatment, and management of complex diseases (Guglielmi, 2023). This includes the creation of large-scale clinical databases, the development of predictive models and decision support systems, and the implementation of remote monitoring and telemedicine services.

To support this digital transformation, the reform calls for significant investments in research infrastructure, including high-performance computing facilities, data storage and management systems, and advanced imaging and diagnostic equipment (Gazzella Ufficiale, 2022). IRCCS are encouraged to collaborate with industry partners and technology providers to develop and validate new digital health solutions while also ensuring the privacy and security of patient data (Guglielmi, 2023).

Another key aspect of the reform is the emphasis on talent development and international collaboration. IRCCS are expected to attract and retain the best researchers and clinicians from around the world by offering competitive salaries, state-of-the-art facilities, and opportunities for career advancement (Guglielmi, 2023). The reform introduces new measures to support the career development of young researchers, such as dedicated funding programs and mentorship initiatives, with the aim of creating a pipeline of future scientific leaders (Gazzella Ufficiale, 2022).

To foster international collaboration, the reform encourages IRCCS to participate in global research networks and consortia (Gazzella Ufficiale, 2022), such as the International Cancer Genome Consortium (ICGC) and the Global Alliance for Genomics and Health (GA4GH). These collaborations enable IRCCS to contribute to large-scale international research projects, share expertise and resources, and gain access to cutting-edge technologies and datasets (Guglielmi, 2023).

Finally, the reform recognizes the importance of patient engagement and public outreach in shaping the future of healthcare research. IRCCS are expected to involve patients and their families in the design and conduct of research studies, ensuring that their needs and priorities are taken into account (Guglielmi, 2023). This might include the creation of patient advisory boards, the development of patient-reported outcome measures (Banfi & Pennestrì, 2023), and the dissemination of research findings to the general public.

Therefore, the future of IRCCS is characterized by an even stronger commitment to excellence, innovation, and patient-centeredness. The recent reform provides a framework for IRCCS to strengthen their role as leaders in biomedical research and healthcare delivery while also promoting collaboration, talent development, and public engagement. By embracing these challenges and opportunities, IRCCS have the potential to drive significant advances in the prevention, diagnosis, and treatment of complex diseases, ultimately improving the health and well-being of patients in Italy and beyond.

The Fondazione Mondino, the focus of our case study, is a prime example of an IRCCS specializing in neurology and neuroscience. As a leading research and healthcare institution in its field, Fondazione Mondino embodies the mission and values of the IRCCS, striving to integrate scientific excellence with patient-centered care. Moreover, it is well-positioned to contribute to the future of IRCCS, leveraging its expertise and resources to develop innovative approaches to patient engagement and care while advancing the frontiers of scientific knowledge in its field. Its participation as one of the IRCCS included in the RIN network highlights its fundamental importance, and its focus on the patient side makes it a compelling case for our analysis.

3.2.5 The Importance of Lombardy in the Italian Healthcare System

Lombardy, Italy's largest region, plays a pivotal role in the country's healthcare system. With a population of around ten million inhabitants, Lombardy has been delivering high-quality health services in accordance with the principles of universal health coverage (UHC) (Signorelli et al., 2020). The region's economic and political significance within Italy further underscores its importance in shaping the national healthcare landscape (Signorelli et al., 2024).

Lombardy's regional health service is characterized by a purchaser-provider split and a strong emphasis on market competition among healthcare providers. The regional health service is organized into health protection agencies (ATS—instead of ASL, local health authorities) and health territorial authorities (ASST—instead of AO, hospital/healthcare organizations), which are responsible for planning, purchasing, and providing healthcare services, respectively (Garattini et al., 2022). One of the most striking features of the healthcare system in this region is the high number of acute hospitals. In total, there are 132 acute care hospitals, of which 78 are public and 54 are private accredited hospitals (Signorelli et al., 2024). Further highlighting its importance, Lombardy is home to 20 IRCCS, 5 of which are public and

15 privates. Overall, Lombardy's hospital infrastructure comprises 55% (83 out of 152) public and 45% private facilities (Maresso et al., 2023; Signorelli et al., 2024).

Lombardy's contribution to the Italian healthcare system is substantial. The region accounts for a significant share of the national healthcare expenditure, value added, and employment. In 2019, Lombardy's healthcare expenditure amounted to €20.5 billion, representing approximately 22% of the total national healthcare expenditure (Signorelli et al., 2024). Moreover, the region's healthcare sector generates a considerable portion of the value added and employment in the country's healthcare industry (Assolombarda, 2022).

Lombardy also plays a crucial role in driving innovation and research in the healthcare sector. The presence of numerous universities, research centers, and life sciences clusters in the region fosters a unique ecosystem for medical research and technological advancements (Assolombarda, 2022). As previously mentioned, the IRCCSs, in particular, are at the forefront of cutting-edge research, attracting top talent and collaborating with international partners to push the boundaries of medical knowledge.

The region's commitment to excellence in healthcare is also expressed in the presence of an important pharmaceutical industry. In Lombardy, there is a significant portion of the Italian pharmaceutical industry, with a value added per capita higher than other European benchmark regions (e.g., Baden-Württemberg, Cataluña, and Île de France) (Assolombarda, 2022). The region's pharmaceutical exports have also shown strong growth over the last decade, although the pandemic has slowed this growth compared to other regions that, instead, have pickup (Assolombarda, 2022).

Challenges and Opportunities in Lombardy's Healthcare System

Despite its strengths, Lombardy's healthcare system faced significant challenges during the COVID-19 pandemic. The region was one of the hardest-hit areas in Italy, with a high number of cases (Plagg et al., 2021). The pandemic exposed some weaknesses in the system, such as the fragmentation of primary care services and the lack of coordination between hospitals and territorial services (Parotto et al., 2023; Plagg et al., 2021).

The pandemic also highlighted the importance of strengthening primary healthcare and investing in community and territorial services to reduce the burden on hospitals (Plagg et al., 2021). The neglect of primary healthcare, with a comparatively low availability of general practitioners per inhabitant in Lombardy, coupled with the initial prioritization of hospitals during the pandemic while overcoming primary healthcare in terms of personal protective equipment and testing resources, contributed to the overwhelming of the hospitals(Plagg et al., 2021). Flexible public healthcare services working in cooperation with general practitioners seems to show better efficiency in containing viral spread and in managing patients (Plagg et al., 2021).

Looking ahead, Lombardy has the opportunity to build on its strengths and address the identified weaknesses to further enhance its healthcare system.

Therefore, by fostering greater collaboration between community and hospital services, promoting patient-centered care, and leveraging its research capabilities, the region can continue to lead the way in delivering high-quality, efficient, and innovative healthcare services.

Lombardy's unique characteristics and challenges make it an ideal context for studying patient engagement and organizational efficiency in the healthcare sector. The region's mix of public and private providers, its strong research infrastructure, and its ongoing efforts to integrate community and hospital services provide a rich environment for exploring innovative approaches to patient-centered care. Moreover, given Lombardy's important role in the Italian healthcare landscape, the findings from Fondazione Mondino case study have the potential to inform policy and practice at both regional and national levels. By understanding the factors that contribute to successful patient engagement and organizational efficiency in this specific context, lessons can be drawn for the broader Italian healthcare system, ultimately contributing to the improvement of patient outcomes and the sustainability of the system as a whole.

3.3 Fondazione Mondino IRCSS

Fondazione Mondino has a rich history that spans over a century of dedication to neurological care and research. The institution's origins can be traced back to the early twentieth century, when Professor Casimiro Mondino, a renowned Italian psychiatrist, laid the foundation for what would become a world-class center for the study and treatment of neurological disorders. Professor Mondino founded an institute, the Neuropathological Clinic, for the "treatment of nervous diseases" (Mondino website) that was established as a legal entity in 1917. Driven by a vision to create a specialized institution that would combine clinical excellence with innovative research, Professor Mondino's legacy has shaped the trajectory of the institution to this day.

3.3.1 Organizational Background

Over the decades, Fondazione Mondino has kept on evolving, adapting to the changing landscape of healthcare while remaining dedicated to its commitment to patient care and scientific advancements. In 1973, the organization achieved a significant milestone when it was officially recognized as an IRCCS by the Italian Ministry of Health. This title further emphasized Fondazione Mondino's position as a leading institution in the field of neuroscience, acknowledging its dual role as a center for the treatment of neurological diseases and a hub for groundbreaking research.

To achieve its objectives regarding a strong integration between research, patient care, and education, Fondazione Mondino collaborates with the University of Pavia through specific agreements. As part of this partnership, Fondazione Mondino hosts the Faculty of Medicine and Surgery; the school of specialization in neurology, child neuropsychiatry, and forensic medicine; and the schools of neurotherapy and psychomotor therapy of developmental age, neurophysiopathology technician, and speech therapy.

As the institution grew in size and reputation, it continued to expand its facilities and services to meet the evolving needs of patients and the scientific community. The hospital, which forms the core of Fondazione Mondino's clinical operations, has undergone numerous renovations and expansions over the years. These developments have enabled the healthcare organization to offer state-of-the-art diagnostic and therapeutic services, aiming for patients to receive the highest quality of care in a well-equipped setting.

In addition to its clinical offerings, Fondazione Mondino has consistently invested in its research infrastructure and capabilities. The institution has established itself as a leader in neurological research, with a focus on translational medicine. Translational medicine, also known as translational science, is a branch of medical research that aims to bridge the gap between basic science and clinical application (Wehling, 2021). Through collaborations with leading universities, research institutes, and industry partners, Fondazione Mondino offers a rich research ecosystem that drives innovation and advancements in the field of neuroscience.

Fondazione Mondino is the evidence of the enduring vision of its founder and the dedication of the professionals who have contributed to its growth and success. The organization's history is a story of resilience, adaptability, and a continuous commitment to improving the lives of those affected by neurological disorders. This is reflected in the Fondazione Mondino's mission, which is summarized in offering "care, research, training, and innovation in neurosciences."

3.3.2 Organizational Structure and Governance

Fondazione Mondino boasts a robust and well-defined organizational structure that has the aim of ensuring efficient operation, effective decision-making, and accountability at all levels. The institution's governance is designed to integrate clinical care, research, and education in a seamless way, as it has to best reflect its status as a Scientific Institute for Research, Hospitalization, and Healthcare (IRCCS) dedicated to advancing the field of neuroscience.

At the apex of the organization is the Board of Directors, led by a President. Demonstrating the close ties between Fondazione Mondino and the academic world, the President of the Board is the Rector of the University of Pavia. This appointment underscores the healthcare organization's commitment to fostering strong links between clinical practice and academic research. Moreover, the Vice President's role is filled by the Prorector, further underscoring the important relationship between Fondazione Mondino and the university.

The Board is composed of esteemed professionals from various fields, including academia, healthcare, and business. This diverse composition ensures a rich tapestry of perspectives and expertise in guiding the organization's strategic direction. The Board is responsible for setting the organization's long-term vision, approving budgets, and ensuring adherence to its mission and values. Regular meetings of the Board are organized to review performance, discuss strategic initiatives, and take key decisions that shape the future of the organization.

The executive leadership of Fondazione Mondino is divided among three key figures: the General Director, the Scientific Director, and the Health Director. This triumvirate, which represent the College of Directors, works in close collaboration to oversee the day-to-day operations and strategic direction of the institution. Their synergistic relationship ensures a balanced approach that considers clinical, scientific, and administrative perspectives in all major decisions.

The General Director (sometimes referred to as General Manager), appointed by the Board of Directors, is responsible for the overall management of the institution. This role requires a strong background in management and a proven track record of leadership positions in complex organizations. The General Director oversees the institution's ordinary management, functional organization, and is accountable for achieving the general objectives set by the Board of Directors. They are delegated the implementation of initiatives outlined in the annual budget approved by the Board, as well as the organization of personnel as defined in the organizational act.

The Scientific Director, working alongside the General Director, is appointed by the Board of Directors on the President's proposal, after consulting with the General Director. The role requires a distinguished expert in neuroscience, with high scientific and managerial capabilities acquired through top positions in public or private research institutions. Working closely with the Board and the General Director, the Scientific Director develops, promotes, and implements the research strategy to ensure that the research objectives are achieved. This includes taking care of external collaborations with other research institutions, universities, and industry partners, as well as checking that research conducted at Fondazione Mondino meets the highest standards of scientific excellence and ethical integrity. Therefore, they are responsible for coordinating, directing, and overseeing scientific and research activities, as well as securing funding to meet established goals. The Scientific Director manages the research budget allocated by the General Director, following the programmatic and accounting guidelines approved by the Board of Directors.

Completing the College of Directors is the Health Director, who also serves as the Medical Director of the hospital. Appointed by the Board of Directors on the President's proposal and with the General Director's input, this role underscores once again the integration of clinical care and research at the IRCCS. The Health Director is responsible for overseeing clinical operations and supporting the delivery of high-quality patient care while ensuring compliance with healthcare regulations and best practices.

These three Directors collectively form the strategic management of the institution. Their meetings organized regularly—often weekly—serve as moments for studying, developing, and sharing actions and projects for the institute, including

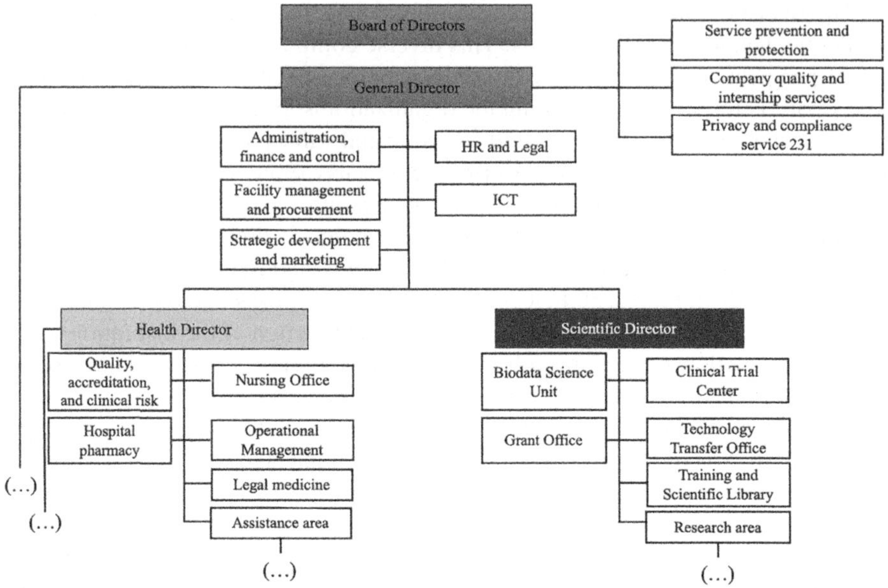

Fig. 3.2 Organizational structure. *Source*: adapted from the organizational act of Fondazione Mondino (Mondino website)

operational directives for various levels of execution. The College of Directors also formulates opinions and proposals for the President and the Board of Directors (Fig. 3.2).

Fondazione Mondino's organizational structure is further divided into several areas:

- *Complex operating units* are internal organizational divisions in the technical-administrative or care delivery domains, each led by a Director.
- *Simple operating units* are subdivisions of the complex units.
- *Research units* conduct preclinical and clinical research across multiple subtopics within a specific thematic area. They involve personnel from various institutions (Fondazione Mondino, the University of Pavia, or IUSS) and are directed by employed or affiliated medical staff.
- *Research sections* focus on preclinical or clinical research in specific thematic areas with full scientific autonomy. They are not hierarchically bound to any center and typically do not include staff from multiple institutions.
- *Offices, services, and operational groups* provide various support functions across the organization.
- *Centers* are specialized units of excellence equipped with cutting-edge technologies and staffed by experienced professionals. They integrate diagnostic, treatment, and translational clinical research activities in specific pathological areas. In particular, these centers also serve as training hubs for doctors, researchers, and nurses, ensuring the integration of care activities with training and research.

The healthcare organization also emphasizes interdepartmental collaboration through its matrix structure, which allows for the formation of multidisciplinary teams to address complex challenges and drive innovation. Regular meetings and communication channels are organized and available to the members in order to facilitate coordination across different departments and functions.

Furthermore, Fondazione Mondino places a strong emphasis on transparency and accountability. The organization has implemented systems for monitoring and evaluating its performance, including regular audits, quality assurance programs, and patient satisfaction surveys. Specifically, two control bodies have been established: One, the single auditor, is appointed by the Board of Directors from among registered legal auditors to monitor the organization's compliance with laws and ethical standards. Then, there is the Supervisory Board, composed of three members, only one of which is internal from Fondazione Mondino. The role is to monitor Fondazione Mondino to ensure prevention for the organization and its members from crimes that could lead to administrative liability.

Recently, Fondazione Mondino has also been actively involved in the development of an Intercompany Department of Neuroscience, a functional collaboration with other healthcare institutions in the region. This initiative aims to enhance patient care by creating integrated care pathways and fostering research collaborations across institutions.

Through this comprehensive organizational structure and governance model, Fondazione Mondino has created a framework that enables it to effectively pursue its mission of advancing neurological care, research, and education while remaining adaptable to evolving healthcare challenges and opportunities.

Organizational Structure of Clinical and Research Activities

Fondazione Mondino is renowned for its expertise in a wide range of neurological disorders, offering comprehensive diagnostic, therapeutic, and rehabilitative services to patients from across Italy and beyond. In fact, building on its robust organizational structure, Fondazione Mondino has developed a comprehensive approach to neurological care and research that sets it apart in the field of neuroscience. This approach is characterized by a seamless integration of clinical practice, cutting-edge research, and advanced education.

At the heart of Fondazione Mondino's clinical care structure lies a multifaceted approach to neurological disorders. The *Emergency Neurology* area exemplifies this, operating across two hospital centers—Fondazione Mondino and Policlinico San Matteo, both IRCCS and both in Pavia, Italy. This innovative dual-center model allows for a more responsive and comprehensive emergency neurological service. It encompasses a Level II Stroke Unit[1] at San Matteo and a Level I Stroke Unit at Mondino, complemented by round-the-clock neurologist presence in the emergency department. This setup was developed to reach rapid, specialized care for stroke patients, which is crucial for minimizing long-term neurological damage.

The *Elective Neurology* area forms the backbone of Fondazione Mondino's specialized neurological care. With 60 beds, it caters to a diverse range of neurological conditions, from behavioral to movement disorders. The area is divided into specialized units, each focusing on specific neurological diseases. For instance, the *Behavioral Neurology Unit* addresses cognitive and behavioral disorders, while the *Parkinson's Disease and Movement Disorders Unit* offers advanced treatments including deep brain stimulation. This structure allows for highly tailored care while maintaining the flexibility to adapt to evolving patient needs.

Fondazione Mondino's commitment to comprehensive care extends to pediatric patients through its *Child Neuropsychiatry Unit*. This unit not only provides acute care but also offers rehabilitation services and extensive outpatient support, ensuring a continuum of care from diagnosis through to community reintegration. The institution's focus on rehabilitation is further emphasized in its *Adult Rehabilitation* area, which employs a multidisciplinary approach to provide personalized rehabilitation programs.

The outpatient services at Fondazione Mondino are organized in a way that it provides easy access to specialized care. The separation of adult and pediatric clinics, along with dedicated spaces for specific projects, allows for efficient patient flow and specialized care delivery. Such an organization extends also to the diagnostic services, where state-of-the-art technology supports both clinical care and research activities. Figure 4.2 summarizes the organizational structure of Fondazione Mondino when it comes to the clinical area.

When it comes to research, Fondazione Mondino has adopted a very specific, yet dynamic structure. The institution has established several specialized research units, each focusing on critical areas of neuroscience. From digital neuroscience to pediatric neuroscience, these units conduct both preclinical and clinical research, truly fostering the translational approach that bridges research and laboratory findings with clinical applications. This structure not only allows for focused expertise but also promotes cross-unit collaboration, which is an essential tool for addressing complex neurological issues.

A specific characteristic of Fondazione Mondino's approach is its innovative *Center* model. These centers of excellence integrate clinical care, research, and education in specific neurological areas. For example, the *Dementia Center* brings

---

[1] Stroke Units are specialized hospital units dedicated to the care of stroke patients. Level I Stroke Units provide essential stroke care, which includes acute treatment and early rehabilitation. Level II Stroke Units offer more advanced care which entails complex interventions and management of more severe cases. They typically have more specialized staff and equipment, allowing them to handle a wider range of stroke complications. Therefore, the Level II Unit at Policlinico San Matteo IRCCS can manage more complex cases, while the Level I Unit at Fondazione Mondino handles less severe cases and provides follow-up care.

Table 3.7 List of centers. *Source*: adapted from the organizational act of Fondazione Mondino (Mondino Website—Organizational act)

Center	Clinical care	Research
Dementia	C.U. Behavior neurology	Dementia Unit
Parkinson's Disease / Movement Disorders	C.U. Parkinson and movement disorders C.U. General Neurology	Movement Disorders Unit
Sleep medicine	S.U. Sleep medicine	Sleep Medicine and Epilepsy Section
Epilepsy	S.U. Study and clinical care of Epilepsy and EEG service	Sleep Medicine and Epilepsy Section
Multiple Sclerosis / Neuroimmunology	S.U. Multiple sclerosis and demyelinating diseases	Multiple sclerosis unit
Child Neuropsychiatry	C.U. Child Neuropsychiatry	Pediatric neurosciences unit
Headache	C.U. Headache Diagnosis and Treatment	Headache and Neurorehabilitation Unit
Neurogenetics	C.U. Medical Genetics Laboratory	Neurogenetics Unit
Neurorehabilitation	C.U. Neurorehabilitation	Headache and Neurorehabilitation Unit
Neuroimaging	C.U. Radiology and Imaging Diagnostics	Advanced Imaging and Artificial Intelligence Unit
Psychology	Adult Clinical Psychology Service Child and Adolescent Clinical Psychology Service	
Cerebrovascular Diseases	C.U. Type B Semi-Intensive - Level I Stroke Unit	
Neurooncology	C.U. Neurooncology and Neuroinflammation	

together clinicians studying cognitive disorders, researchers investigating novel treatments, and professors training the next generation of specialists. This model facilitates rapid translation of research findings into clinical practice, ensures that clinical observations inform research directions, and provides rich training grounds for future professionals. A list of centers is presented in Table 3.7.

Fondazione Mondino's influence extends far beyond its internal organization thanks to the numerous strategic collaborations and network participations. The institution plays a crucial role as a neurological hub for the Pavia district and is an integral part of the regional *Emergency and Urgency Network*. Its involvement in the *Intercompany Department of Neurosciences* represents an innovative approach to healthcare collaboration, aiming to enhance patient care through integrated care pathways and foster inter-institutional research collaborations.

On a broader scale, Fondazione Mondino's participation in national and international networks, such as the National IRCCS Network for Neuroscience and Rehabilitation (RIN) and the European Reference Network for Rare and Complex Epilepsies, enhances its research capabilities and contributes to recognize and maintain its status as a leader in the field of neuroscience.

As previously mentioned, the organization's commitment to advancing neuroscience also extends to education and training. As a teaching hospital affiliated with the University of Pavia's Faculty of Medicine and Surgery, Fondazione Mondino hosts several specialty schools and degree programs in neuroscience-related fields.

Fondazione Mondino has created a comprehensive ecosystem where clinical care, research, and education are deeply linked. This integrated approach allows the healthcare organization to provide cutting-edge neurological care, drive innovations in research, and train the younger neurological specialists.

3.3.3 Organization's Mission, Vision, and Strategic Lines

Fondazione Mondino's mission and vision embody a comprehensive approach to neuroscience that has evolved over the years. At its core, the institution is dedicated to advancing neurological care through a multifaceted strategy encompassing patient care, scientific research, professional education, and technological innovation. This holistic approach reflects a deep understanding of the interconnected nature of these elements and their importance in the advancement of neuroscience.

As Fondazione Mondino looks to the future, it envisions itself as a leading institution recognized for its excellence in neuroscience, not just within Italy but worldwide. This vision is built on several key points that align with the rapidly evolving landscape of healthcare and, more specifically, neuroscience research. The organization recognizes that the future of neurological care lies in personalized medicine, innovative research, technological advancements, and the seamless integration of diverse expertise.

To realize this vision, Fondazione Mondino has outlined a series of strategic objectives that demonstrate its commitment to innovation and excellence. A crucial aspect of this strategy is the continued strengthening of the synergy between clinical practice, research endeavors, and specialized training programs. This integration, which has been a specific key driver of the institution for over a hundred years, is seen as fundamentally important for applying translational research, thus ensuring that research findings translate into improved patient outcomes, and that clinical observations truly inform new research directions.

Fondazione Mondino's strategy emphasizes the importance of technology transfer and open innovation. The organization is actively working to bridge the gap between academic research and practical applications, collaborating with a wide range of partners in the healthcare ecosystem. The institution is highlighting the fundamental role that an open innovation philosophy and approach could play on this regard. Therefore, Fondazione Mondino recognizes that groundbreaking and radical discoveries often stem from unexpected collaborations and cross-disciplinary approaches. This willingness to venture beyond traditional boundaries reflects a forward-thinking mindset essential for addressing complex challenges in such rapid changing environment.

Interestingly, Fondazione Mondino is not just focused on scientific and medical advancements but also on broader societal issues. The organization, in fact, is committed to implementing sustainable practices across its operations, investing in eco-friendly technologies, and promoting policies that foster inclusion and gender equality. These initiatives highlight a first proper step of the organization toward recognizing the importance of the existing links among environmental, economic, and social factors in healthcare.

At the heart of Fondazione Mondino's strategy is a strong commitment to patient-centered care. This approach is evident in several key areas. The institution is leveraging big data analytics to develop increasingly personalized treatment plans, recognizing that each patient's neurological condition is unique. This data-driven approach will integrate information from biological markers, imaging studies, and psychosocial indicators to provide tailored prevention strategies, precise diagnoses, and customized treatment and rehabilitation programs.

The emphasis on patient-centered care also includes the importance field of digital health. Fondazione Mondino has recently been actively integrating digital and mobile technologies to enhance patient engagement and care delivery. These innovations range from the introduction of an app for improving back and front office services to telemedicine platforms that improve access to specialized neurological care. There will be other advancements, like digital therapies that complement traditional treatment approaches. By embracing these and new upcoming technologies, the organization aims to create a more connected and responsive healthcare ecosystem.

Perhaps most significantly, Fondazione Mondino is reimagining its organizational and relational models to put patients at the center. This involves a comprehensive redesign of processes and interactions, shifting focus from a disease-centric model to one that prioritizes the needs and experiences of patients. Importantly, this redesign is not happening in isolation; patients and other stakeholders are actively involved in shaping these new models. The integration of digital technologies, such as remote monitoring systems, will further support this patient-centered approach by enabling personalized care.

The institution's commitment to patient-centered care is also reflected in its approach to team organization. Fondazione Mondino is moving towards a model of multi-professional, cross-functional teams that bring together clinicians, researchers, technicians, nurses, and administrative staff. This approach ensures that patients benefit from a diverse range of expertise and perspectives, leading to more comprehensive and coordinated care.

3.3.4 Organizational Efficiency at Fondazione Mondino

As highlighted in the first chapter of this book, in healthcare organizations, efficiency is defined as the ability to optimize health outcomes by allocating available resources effectively (Gyrd-Hansen, 2014). For specialized institutions like Fondazione Mondino, this involves strategically managing workforce, capital, and other resources to enhance both healthcare services and research output while controlling costs (Cylus et al., 2016; Laurance et al., 2014). Efficiency in this context includes technical, production, and allocative aspects, aiming to improve health outcomes, reduce costs, and enhance treatment effectiveness (Tehrani & Meckl-Sloan, 2016).

One of the ways to assess Fondazione Mondino's efficiency is by examining various financial and operational indicators. Therefore, we examine indicators gathered from the organization's 2021, 2022, and 2023 balance sheets which are publicly available, allowing us to observe trends and changes over time.

Financial Stability and Organization's Liquidity

The balance sheets offer recent insights into Fondazione Mondino's financial stability. Here follows a recap of the main indicators derived from the financial reports from 2021 to 2023 (Table 3.8).

The equity amount represents 42.26% of the total liabilities and equity. It has improved consistently over the 3 years, representing a 0.67 percentage point increase from 41.59% in 2021. This indicator is important as it underscores a strong—and improved—financial foundation. Such a robust equity base offers to the organization the chance to self-finance operations and investments, which in turn contributes to long-term stability and efficiency.

Table 3.8 Fondazione Mondino balance sheet summary, 2021–2023 (in €). *Source*: adapted from the publicly available financial reports

	2021	2022	2023
Assets			
Total Fixed Assets	18,944,213	18,250,440	19,218,663
Total Current Assets	24,012,924	25,389,185	26,585,694
Prepayments and Accrued	1,745,731	906,205	1,369,744
Total Assets	44,702,868	44,545,830	47,174,102
Liabilities and Equity			
Equity	18,594,367	19,138,833	19,937,205
Provisions for Risks	3,003,232	3,717,755	3,663,472
Employees Severance	2,263,581	1,913,181	1,691,197
Debts	18,907,909	18,075,444	19,341,563
Accruals and Deferred	1,933,779	1,700,618	2,540,666
Total Liabilities and Equity	44,702,868	44,545,830	47,174,102

A key indicator of short-term efficiency is liquidity. It can be assessed through the current ratio, which is calculated as current assets divided by current liabilities. This indicator measures the organization's ability to pay off its short-term liabilities with its short-term assets. In Fondazione Mondino, the current ratio has fluctuated in the 3 years under evaluation. While in 2021 the ratio was 1.46, in 2022, it reached 1.57 to then slightly decrease in 2023 counting 1.38.

Despite the decrease in 2023, the ratio still suggests that Fondazione Mondino has adequate liquidity to meet its short-term obligations. In other words, for every euro of current liabilities, in 2023, Fondazione Mondino has 1.38 € in current assets. Therefore, a slight decrease in the current ratio is not a sign of a "not efficient" organization; rather, it should represent a warning to keep on monitoring the ratio in order to ensure continued financial flexibility.

Strategic Investments

Efficient organizations invest strategically to enhance future capabilities. Fondazione Mondino pattern of investments from 2021 to 2023 reflects what seems to be a strategic approach to enhance its long-term capabilities (Table 3.9).

Total investment in fixed assets in 2023, which reach the amount of 2,712,237 €, includes an investment in a high-technology platform funded by the Ministry of Health, which amounts to 2,281,400 €.

These investments show an important increase in 2023 compared to previous years. However, the fluctuation in investment levels might reflect a cyclical approach, where major investments are made periodically rather than each year. While increasing short-term costs, these investments can significantly improve long-term efficiency by enhancing, for example, and in the case of the high-technology platform, diagnostic, and treatment capabilities.

The investment pattern reflects a good equilibrium between maintaining current operations and investing in future capabilities, especially if we consider the up and downs in research funding as previously shown.

However, it is also important to bear in mind that, in the healthcare sector, the return on such investments often includes improved patient outcomes and research capabilities, which are challenging to quantify financially in the short term. Future

Table 3.9 Total investment in fixed assets. *Source*: adapted from publicly available financial reports of Fondazione Mondino

Year	Total investment in fixed assets
2021	1,643,158
2022	997,838
2023	2,712,237

evaluations might want to attempt measuring the impact of these investments both on research efficiency and output and on patient care.

Revenue Growth and Cost Management

We have stated that efficient healthcare organizations should demonstrate their ability to grow revenues while at the same time controlling for costs (Lewandowski, 2023). On this matter, Fondazione Mondino's income statements (see Appendix B for details) reveal interesting indicators. Table 3.10 provides a summary of the income statement's voices needed for the purpose of this specific analysis.

The organization has shown revenue growth over the considered 3-year period. While production costs have increased at a slightly higher rate, the recovery in the operating profit and EBIT margin from 2022 to 2023 suggests improved efficiency in the latest year.

Indeed, the fact that revenue growth outpaced the increase in cost indicates that Fondazione Mondino has put into practice an effective cost management, which should be considered as one of the key aspects of organizational efficiency. As a further proof of the efficient management of the organization in the last year is the improved operating profit (EBIT—Earnings Before Interests and Taxes) that reached 1,076,637€ in 2023, up from 615,453€ in 2022. The EBIT margin improved from 1.24% to 2.05% of total revenue, demonstrating enhanced operational efficiency in the last fiscal year. This increase suggests that the organization has become more efficient in its core operations.

Research Efficiency

Healthcare organization's efficiency covers various aspects, and—especially in the case of an IRCCS—the research efficiency is of fundamental importance. It refers to the ability to produce and publish high-quality research outputs with optimal allocation and use of resources. For organizations like Fondazione Mondino, this is

Table 3.10 Revenue and cost comparison, 2021–2023 (in €). *Source*: adapted from the publicly available financial reports of Fondazione Mondino

	2021	2022	2023	1-year change (2023 - 2022)	2-year change (2023 - 2021)
Total Revenue	47,784,349	49,605,860	52,618,852	6.07%	10.12%
Production Costs	45,976,099	48,990,407	51,542,215	5.21%	12.11%
Operating Profit	1,808,250	615,453	1,076,637	74.9%	-40.46%
EBIT margin	3.78%	1.24%	2.05%	0.81%	-1.73%

a fundamental aspect as it reflects on their mission as research healthcare organizations.

Fondazione Mondino's research efficiency has been analyzed using several key metrics, including the number of publications per unit of funding (research efficiency ratio), the funding required per publication, and the impact factor per unit of funding. These metrics offer quite a good perspective on how effectively the organization is utilizing its research funding. It is crucial to acknowledge that the data for 2021 might be biased due to the higher number of publications related to COVID-19 topics, as Fondazione Mondino, being an excellence in its field, significantly contributed to research in this period.

Still, in the last 3 years, from 2021 to 2023, Fondazione Mondino has demonstrated resilience and adaptability in its research activities as summarized in Table 3.11.

According to the 2023 financial report, Fondazione Mondino experienced a significant reduction in research funding of about 28.8% compared to 2022. Despite this cut, the financial report indicates that scientific productivity remained stable. This shown stability, despite the reduced funding, might in fact suggest an increase in research efficiency.

To quantify the research efficiency, we calculated the research efficiency ratio, which measures the number of publications produced per euro of funding. This indicator fluctuated over the 3-year period. In 2021, the ratio was 0.000112, indicating that the organization produced 0.000112 publications for each euro of funding received. This ratio decreased to 0.000068 in 2022 but improved to 0.000093 in 2023. The fluctuation suggests changes in the effectiveness of converting funding into publications. The lower ratio in 2022 could reflect a normalization after the surge in COVID-19-related publications in 2021, while the improvement in 2023 seems to indicate a recovery in efficiency, possibly due to better resource allocation and management strategies.

The funding required to produce a single publication increased significantly from €8927.9 in 2021 to €14,655.3 in 2022, mostly indicating reduced efficiency. However, this cost decreased to €10,712.1 in 2023, reflecting an improvement but still not reaching the 2021 levels. The increased cost in 2022 may be attributed to a focus on fewer but potentially more resource-intensive research projects, while the

Table 3.11 Research efficiency (2021–2023). *Source*: adapted from publicly available Fondazione Mondino financial reports

Year	Research contribution (€)	Publications (number)	Impact Factor (IF)	Research efficiency ratio	Funding per publication (€)
2021	2,848,000	319	1549.93	0.000112	8,927.9
2022	3,869,000	264	1329.73	0.000068	14,655.3
2023	2,753,000	257	1238.07	0.000093	10,712.1

improvement in 2023 suggests better control over research expenses and more effective use of funding.

Yet, the overall decrease in the total impact factor at Fondazione Mondino from 1549.93 in 2021 to 1238.07 in 2023 highlights some significant trends and challenges. The high impact factor in 2021 was likely influenced by the surge in publications related to COVID-19, which attracted substantial global attention and citations. As the urgency of COVID-19 research declined, the focus may have shifted back to more specialized or routine areas of neurological research, which do not attract the same level of citations. Additionally, there may be a citation lag for more recent publications from 2022 and 2023, which have not yet had sufficient time to accumulate significant citations. This effect suggests that the true impact of recent research might not yet be fully reflected in the current metrics.

Finally, it is important to note that these simple proxies of efficiency do not capture the full complexity of research output and related efficiency. A more comprehensive assessment would include factors such as publication quality (e.g., analyzing the journals in which research is published) and long-term research outcomes that help in evaluating how the research translates into improved treatments or diagnostic methods. Unfortunately, these pieces of information are not currently available to the authors.

Healthcare Service Efficiency

In addition to financial stability and research efficiency, it is crucial to assess the efficiency of Fondazione Mondino in delivering healthcare services to its patients. This aspect of efficiency is central to the organization's mission as a healthcare provider. Table 3.12 summarizes the four indicators identified to measure this type of efficiency.

The first indicator is represented by the average length of stay (ALOS) for patients. A shorter ALOS generally indicates more efficient use of hospital resources and faster patient recovery (e.g., Vinh et al., 2019). At Fondazione Mondino, the ALOS decreased from 9.8 days in 2021 to 9.4 days in 2023. This decrease suggests improved efficiency in patient care and resource management, possibly due to the optimization of treatment protocols and the adoption of best practices in healthcare delivery.

Table 3.12 Healthcare service efficiency indicators (2021–2023)

Year	Average length of stay	Bed occupancy rate	Outpatients visits per day	Extra-regional patients
2021	9.8	72.9%	280	33.7%
2022	9.6	72.9%	277	32.8%
2023	9.4	74.3%	309	35.1%

Another important indicator is the bed occupancy rate, which measures the proportion of available hospital beds that are occupied by patients in a specific period (e.g., He et al., 2019). A higher occupancy rate generally indicates more efficient use of hospital infrastructure, but it should not exceed 85% to be ready for emergency patients (Moengin et al., 2014). Fondazione Mondino showed an increase in the bed occupancy rate from 72.9% in 2021 and 2022 to 74.3% in 2023 (Table 3.12). This improvement suggests that the organization has been able to more efficiently manage its patient flow and bed capacity.

The third indicator is the number of outpatient visits per day which also increased—from 280 in 2021 to 309 in 2023 (see Table 3.12)—indicating that Fondazione Mondino has been able to serve a larger number of patients in an ambulatory setting. This increase in outpatient capacity could be attributed to various factors, such as the expansion of outpatient clinics, the streamlining of appointment scheduling, and the adoption of telemedicine solutions.

The proportion of extra-regional patients, the last analyzed indicator, at Fondazione Mondino slightly varied over the 3-year period, from 33.7% in 2021 to 32.8% in 2022, and then increasing to 35.1% in 2023 (see Table 3.12). The relatively high proportion of extra-regional patients suggests that the organization has a strong reputation and attracts patients from beyond its immediate geographical area. The increase in 2023 might indicate an improvement in the organization's ability to attract patients from other regions, possibly due to its enhanced clinical efficiency and quality of care. Extant studies suggest that extra-regional patients represent an unconstrained source of revenue and hospitals may use waiting time and length of stay as levers to attract these patients (Balia et al., 2018).

Patient Satisfaction As a Potential Efficiency Indicator

While financial and operational metrics provide valuable insights into healthcare organizational efficiency, patient satisfaction is an indicator of healthcare quality that could, indeed, affect also the organization's efficiency. Fondazione Mondino conducts regular customer satisfaction surveys for both inpatient and outpatient services. These surveys use a 7-point Likert scale, where 7 represents the highest level of satisfaction with the provided service.

The publicly available surveys cover the last 2 years, 2022 and 2023. The outpatient services survey findings from 2022 with 307 respondents and 2023 with 363 respondents reveal some interesting metrics. Overall satisfaction increased from 6 out of 7 in 2022 to 7 out of 7 in 2023, indicating an improvement in patient experience. The willingness to recommend the facility remained consistently high at 7 out of 7 in both years, suggesting strong patient trust and loyalty. In 2023, several areas achieved excellence with scores of 7 out of 7, including staff courtesy, information received, clarity of explanations, and attention from nursing and technical staff. These areas showed improvement from their 2022 scores of 6 out of 7. Most other aspects of outpatient care, such as appointment booking, waiting times, and facility cleanliness, maintained consistent scores of 6 out of 7 across both years. Interestingly, the attention received from medical staff saw a slight decrease from 7 out of 7 in 2022 to 6 out of 7 in 2023.

For inpatient services, the survey findings from 2022 with only 111 respondents and 2023 with a good sample of 494 respondents still offer an interesting point of view. The overall satisfaction remained stable at 6 out of 7, while the willingness to recommend the facility held steady at the maximum score of 7 out of 7. Both years saw consistently high scores of 7 out of 7 for nursing care, rehabilitation staff, and medical staff, underscoring the strength of Fondazione Mondino's clinical team. Food quality and cleanliness both scored 5 out of 7 in 2023, with food quality showing improvement from its 2022 score of 4 out of 7. An improvement occurred in the information provided at discharge, which improved from 6 out of 7 in 2022 to 7 out of 7 in 2023.

While these results provide a good snapshot of Fondazione Mondino's performance from a patient perspective, it has to be noted that such high results may indicate a bias in the respondents' sample. As a matter of fact, those willing to respond to customers' satisfaction surveys might be those patients that had a particularly positive experience with the organization. On the other hand, those leaving reviews online might instead be a subgroup of patients that had very negative experiences. Thus, in both cases, outliers' feedback might be important to address specific issues, but cannot be those on which such an important organization develops its strategic initiatives.

3.4 Conclusions

The SSN has undergone significant evolution since its establishment in 1978, adapting to changing healthcare needs, economic pressures, and societal expectations. Throughout this evolution, the system's core principles of universality, solidarity, and equity have remained constant, even as its organizational structure and governance have been refined over time.

The decentralized nature of the SSN, with regions playing a crucial role in healthcare delivery, has led to both innovations and challenges. This regional autonomy has allowed for tailored approaches to local health needs but has also resulted in disparities in healthcare access and quality across different parts of the country. The ongoing efforts to balance national standards with regional flexibility remain a key focus of healthcare policy in Italy.

Within this complex landscape, specialized institutions like the IRCCS have emerged as centers of excellence, combining cutting-edge and innovative research with high-quality patient care. These institutes, including Fondazione Mondino, play a crucial role in advancing medical knowledge, developing innovative treatments, and setting standards for healthcare delivery in their respective fields.

The Lombardy region, home to Fondazione Mondino, stands out as a particularly important player in the Italian healthcare system. With its significant concentration of healthcare resources, research institutions, and a mix of public and private providers, Lombardy offers a unique environment for studying healthcare innovation and patient engagement strategies.

Our exploration of Fondazione Mondino reveals an organization that stands as an example of excellence in neurological care, research, and education. Its transformation from a local clinic to a globally recognized center offers valuable lessons on integrating patient-centered care with innovative research and education in neuroscience.

The organizational framework and governance model of Fondazione Mondino showcase how a healthcare institution can balance the demands of the three interconnected areas of care, research, and education. The close collaboration with the University of Pavia, as evidenced also by the leadership roles held by university officials on the Board of Directors, showcases a successful model of academic-clinical partnership that enhances both patient care and advancement in research.

Fondazione Mondino's commitment to patient-centered care, as reflected in its strategic vision and operational practices, might serve as a roadmap for other healthcare institutions aiming to boost patient engagement and outcomes. The focus on personalized medicine, digital health solutions, and multidisciplinary care teams underscores the evolving nature of healthcare delivery in our rapidly changing world.

Furthermore, the institution's emphasis on sustainability, inclusivity, and open innovation demonstrates an understanding that modern healthcare providers must address broader societal issues alongside their core mission. This approach not only offers opportunities to improving Fondazione Mondino's impact on patient care but also contributes to its long-term adaptability and relevance in a dynamic healthcare landscape.

As we move forward to examine more in details some of the patient engagement strategies implemented by Fondazione Mondino, it is clear that these initiatives are built on a solid foundation of institutional excellence mixed with a commitment to improving patient outcomes. The insights derived from the experience of Fondazione Mondino might offer food for thought for healthcare providers, policymakers, and researchers, as they strive to enhance patient engagement and increase the quality of care on a regional or global scale.

References

Armocida, B., Formenti, B., Palestra, F., Ussai, S., & Missoni, E. (2020). COVID-19: Universal health coverage now more than ever. *Journal of Global Health, 10*(1).

Assolombarda. (2022). *The importance of the Life Sciences value chain in Lombardy. Report n°7/2022*. Edited by Economic Research Department and Life Science. Retrieved on May, 2024, https://www.assolombarda.it/centro-studi/the-importance-of-the-life-sciences-value-chain-in-lombardy-2022#:~:text=The%20contribution%20of%20the%20Lombard,accounts%20for%2019.5%25%20of%20the

Bachelet, V. (2008). *Libro bianco sui principi fondamentali del servizio sanitario nazionale*. Libera Università di studi sociali Luiss Guido Carli Centro di ricerca sulle amministrazioni pubbliche.

Balia, S., Brau, R., & Marrocu, E. (2018). Interregional patient mobility in a decentralized healthcare system. *Regional Studies, 52*(3), 388–402. https://doi.org/10.1080/00343404.2017.1307954

Banfi, G., & Pennestrì, F. (2023). *Patient-reported outcome measures to enhance health care*. Edra Publication. ISBN: 9781957260419.

Bartoloni. (2024). *Cure essenziali, metà Regioni non le garantiscono: Veneto al top, male Valle d'Aosta*. Retrieved: February 20, 2024, https://www.ilsole24ore.com/art/cure-essenziali-meta-regioni-non-garantiscono-veneto-top-male-valle-d-aosta-AF1GhNmC?refresh_ce=1

Bordignon, M., Coretti, S., Piacenza, M., & Turati, G. (2020). Hardening subnational budget constraints via administrative subordination: The Italian experience of recovery plans in regional health services. *Health Economics, 29*(11), 1378–1399. https://doi.org/10.1002/hec.4138. Epub 2020 Aug 13. PMID: 32789958.

Bosa, I., Castelli, A., Castelli, M., Ciani, O., Compagni, A., Galizzi, M. M., Garofano, M., Ghislandi, S., Giannoni, M., Marini, G., & Vainieri, M. (2021). Corona-regionalism? Differences in regional responses to COVID-19 in Italy. *Health Policy, 125*(9), 1179–1187.

Broek, S., Buiskool, B. J., Vennekens, A., & van der Horst, R. (2012). *Study on the current situation and prospects of mutuals in Europe*. Final report by European Commission, Project number: BA03954.

Bruzzi, S., Ivaldi, E., & Santagata, M. (2022). Measuring regional performance in the Italian NHS: Are disparities decreasing? *Social Indicators Research, 159*, 1057–1084. https://doi.org/10.1007/s11205-021-02775-8

Chisari, G., & Lega, F. (2023). Impact of austerity programs: Evidence from the Italian national health service. *Health Services Management Research, 36*(2), 145–152. https://doi.org/10.1177/09514848221134473

Cicchetti, A., Giorgio, L., Di Paolo, M. G., Daugbjerg, S. B., Laurita, R., Morandi, F., Tattoli, A., & Villani, L. (2021). *Sustainability and resilience in the Italian health system*. The London School of Economics and Political Science–Partnership for Health System Sustainability and Resilience.

Cinelli, G., & Fattore, G. (2024). The 2022 community-based integrated care reform in Italy: From desiderata to implementation. *Health Policy, 139*, 104943.

Cingolani, M., Scendoni, R., Fedeli, P., & Cembrani, F. (2023). Artificial intelligence and digital medicine for integrated home care services in Italy: Opportunities and limits. *Frontiers in Public Health, 10*, 1095001.

Cylus, J., Papanicolas, I., & Smith, P. C. (Eds.). (2016). *Health system efficiency: How to make measurement matter for policy and management*. European Observatory on Health Systems and Policies.

D'Alema, M., Venier, M., & Licari, G. (2010). Origine, Organizzazione e funzioni del Servizio Sanitario Nazionale in Italia. *Narrare i Gruppi, 5*(2).

Depalo, D. (2019). The side effects on health of a recovery plan in Italy: A nonparametric bounding approach. *Regional Science and Urban Economics, 78*, 103466.

Donatini, A. (2015). The Italian health care system. *International profiles of health care systems*.

Donatini, A. (2020). *International health care system profiles: Italy*. Commonwealth Fund. https://www.commonwealthfund.org/international-health-policy-center/countries/italy

European Commission. (2023a). *State of Health in the EU: Italy Country Health Profile 2023*. https://health.ec.europa.eu/document/download/67cd0b86-b081-4fa5-84a8-f4487e912320_en?filename=2023_chp_it_english.pdf

European Commission. (2023b). *Towards person-centered integrated care in Italy*. Retrieved May, 2024, https://reform-support.ec.europa.eu/what-we-do/health-and-long-term-care/towards-person-centered-integrated-care-italy-0_en

European Union. (2013). *Your social security rights in Italy*. https://ec.europa.eu/employment_social/empl_portal/SSRinEU/Your%20social%20security%20rights%20in%20Italy_en.pdf

Ferrara, L., Zazzera, A., & Tozzi, V. D. (2022). Managing chronic conditions: Lessons learnt from a comparative analysis of seven years' policies for chronic care patients in Italy. *International Journal of Integrated Care, 22*(1).

Ferré, F., de Belvis, A. G., Valerio, L., Longhi, S., Lazzari, A., Fattore, G., Ricciardi, W., & Maresso, A. (2014). Italy: Health system review. *Health Systems in Transition, 16*(4), 1–168. PMID: 25471543.

Ferré, F., Noto, G., & Vola, F. (2018). Italy's health care system and the crisis: Overview of policy actions and their implementation. *Anais do Instituto de Higiene e Medicina Tropical, 17*(suppl. 1), 47–58.

Fina, S., Heider, B., & Prota, F. (2021). Unequal Italy. *Regional Socio-Economic Disparities in Italy.*

France, G., & Taroni, F. (2005). The evolution of health-policy making in Italy. *Journal of Health Politics, Policy and Law, 30*(1–2), 169–188. https://doi.org/10.1215/03616878-30-1-2-169

France, G., Taroni, F., & Donatini, A. (2005). The Italian health-care system. *Health Economics, 14*(Suppl 1), S187–S202. https://doi.org/10.1002/hec.1035. PMID: 16161196.

Garattini, L., Badinella Martini, M., & Zanetti, M. (2022). The Italian NHS at regional level: Same in theory, different in practice. *The European Journal of Health Economics, 23*(1), 1–5.

Gazzella Ufficiale. (2022). DECRETO LEGISLATIVO 23 dicembre 2022, n. 200. Riordino della disciplina degli Istituti di ricovero e cura a carattere scientifico. (22G00208). https://www.gazzettaufficiale.it/eli/id/2022/12/30/22G00208/SG

Genova, A., & Lombardini, S. (2024). General practitioners in front of COVID-19: Italy in European comparative perspective. *Frontiers in Sociology, 9*, 1365517.

Giorgi, C. (2023). A history of Italy's health policy from the republic to the new century. *Modern Italy, 28*(1), 1–17.

Guglielmi, G. (2023). La Riforma degli IRCCS: la valutazione della Ricerca IRCCS. *Mondino Neuro Week*, 2023.

Gyrd-Hansen, D. (2014). *Concepts of efficiency in health care. Encyclopedia of health economics.* Elsevier. https://doi.org/10.1016/B978-0-12-375678-7.00202-9

He, L., Madathil, S. C., Oberoi, A., Servis, G., & Khasawneh, M. T. (2019). A systematic review of research design and modeling techniques in inpatient bed management. *Computers & Industrial Engineering, 127*, 451-466. https://doi.org/10.1016/j.cie.2018.10.033

INPS. (2022). *La storia dell'INPS.* https://www.inps.it/it/it/inps-comunica/la-carta-dei-servizi-dell-inps/informazioni-generali/la-storia-dell-inps.html#:~:text=Nel%201933%20la%20Cassa%20diviene,Istituto%20Nazionale%20della%20Previdenza%20Sociale

Laurance, J., Henderson, S., Howitt, P. J., Matar, M., Al Kuwari, H., Edgman-Levitan, S., & Darzi, A. (2014). Patient engagement: Four case studies that highlight the potential for improved health outcomes and reduced costs. *Health Affairs, 33*(9), 1627–1634.

Legge 833/1978. (1978). LEGGE 23 dicembre 1978, n. 833. https://presidenza.governo.it/USRI/ufficio_studi/normativa/Legge%2023%20dicembre%201978,%20n.%20833.pdf

Lewandowski, R. A. (2023). *Management control in hospitals: A breakthrough approach to improving performance and efficiency.* CRC Press.

Liberati, P. (2003). *Fiscal federalism and national health standards in Italy: Implications for redistribution. I sistemi di welfare tra decentramento regionale e integrazione europea* (pp. 241–273). Franco Angeli.

Lodi, R. (2023). Sviluppo e implementazione delle reti di ricerca degli IRCCS come eccellenza. *Mondino Neuro Week.*

Maresso, A., Waitzberg, R., Tille, F., Litvinova, Y., Pastorino, G., Nathan, N., & Clarke, D. (2023). Engaging the private sector in delivering health care and goods: Governance lessons from the COVID-19 pandemic. In *Engaging the private sector in delivering health care and goods: Governance lessons from the COVID-19 pandemic.* WHO.

Matranga, D., & Maniscalco, L. (2022). Inequality in healthcare utilization in Italy: How important are barriers to access? *International Journal of Environmental Research and Public Health, 19*(3), 1697.

Ministero della Salute. (2019a). *Strengths of the Italian National Health Service*. https://www.salute.gov.it/portale/cureUE/dettaglioContenutiCureUE.jsp?lingua=english&id=3879&area=healcareUE&menu=vuoto

Ministero della Salute. (2019b). *I princìpi del Servizio sanitario nazionale (SSN)*. https://www.salute.gov.it/portale/lea/dettaglioContenutiLea.jsp?lingua=italiano&id=5073&area=Lea&menu=vuoto

Ministero della Salute. (2021). *Mantenimento dell'erogazione dei LEA - Griglia LEA*. Retrieved on May, 2024, https://www.salute.gov.it/portale/lea/dettaglioContenutiLea.jsp?area=Lea&id=4747&lingua=italiano&menu=monitoraggioLea

Ministero della Salute. (2022). *Ricerca corrente. Attività scientifica degli IRCCS*. Retrieved on May, 2024, https://www.salute.gov.it/portale/ricercaSanitaria/dettaglioContenutiRicercaSanitaria.jsp?lingua=italiano&id=2427&area=Ricerca%20sanitaria&menu=corrente

Ministero della Salute. (2023). *Riconoscimento e conferma carattere scientifico IRCCS*. Retrieved on June, 2024, https://www.salute.gov.it/portale/ricercaSanitaria/dettaglioContenutiRicercaSanitaria.jsp?lingua=italiano&id=1487&area=Ricerca%20sanitaria&menu=ssn

Ministero della Salute. (2024a). *Istituti di Ricovero e Cura a Carattere Scientifico - IRCCS*. Retrieved on May, 2024, https://www.salute.gov.it/portale/ricercaSanitaria/dettaglioContenutiRicercaSanitaria.jsp?lingua=italiano&id=794&area=Ricerca%20sanitaria&menu=ssn#:~:text=Gli%20Istituti%20di%20Ricovero%20e,cura%20di%20alta%20specialità%20o

Ministero della Salute. (2024b). *Istituti di Ricovero e Cura a Carattere Scientifico - IRCCS*. Retrieved in June, 2024, https://www.salute.gov.it/portale/ricercaSanitaria/dettaglioContenutiRicercaSanitaria.jsp?lingua=italiano&id=794&area=Ricerca%20sanitaria&menu=ssn&tab=2

Moengin, P., Septiani, W., & Herviana, S. (2014). A discrete-event simulation metho- dology to optimize the number of beds in hospital. In *Proceedings of the world congress on engineering and computer science international conference on modeling, simulation and control 2014* (pp. 902–907).

Mondino Website. *Atto organizzativo*. https://www.mondino.it/wp-content/uploads/2023/04/ATTO_ORGANIZZATIVO_MONDINO.pdf

Mondino Website. *Bilancio (Balance Sheet)* 2021 – 2022 – 2023. https://www.mondino.it/amministrazione-trasparente/

Mondino Website. *Customer satisfaction survey 2022 – 2023*. https://www.mondino.it/amministrazione-trasparente/

Mondino Website. *History*. https://www.mondino.it/storia/

Neri, S. (2019). The Italian national health service after the economic crisis: from decentralization to differentiated federalism. *e-cadernos CES*, (31).

Neri, S. (2020). Più Stato e più Regioni. L'evoluzione della governance del Servizio sanitario nazionale e la pandemia. *Autonomie locali e servizi sociali, 43*(2), 239–255.

Nuti, S., Ferré, F., Seghieri, C., Foresi, E., & Stukel, T. A. (2020). Managing the performance of general practitioners and specialists referral networks: A system for evaluating the heart failure pathway. *Health Policy, 124*(1), 44–51.

Odone, A., Delmonte, D., Scognamiglio, T., & Signorelli, C. (2020). COVID-19 deaths in Lombardy, Italy: Data in context. *The Lancet Public Health, 5*(6), e310.

OECD. (2019). *Italy: Country health profile 2019, state of health in the EU*. OECD Publishing/European Observatory on Health Systems and Policies. https://doi.org/10.1787/cef1e5cb-en

OECD. (2020). *OECD health statistics*. Retrieved May, 2024, https://www.oecd.org/italy/

OECD. (2023). *Ready for the next crisis? Investing in health system resilience, OECD health policy studies*. OECD Publishing. https://doi.org/10.1787/1e53cf80-en

Parlamento Italiano. (1999). Decreto Legislativo 19 giugno 1999, n. 229. "Norme per la razionalizzazione del Servizio sanitario nazionale, a norma dell'articolo 1 della legge 30 novembre 1998, n. 419" pubblicato nella Gazzetta Ufficiale n. 165 del 16 luglio 1999 - Supplemento Ordinario n. 132. https://www.parlamento.it/parlam/leggi/deleghe/99229dl.htm#:~:text=La%20legge%20regionale%20istituisce%20e,delle%20autonomie%20locali%2C%20ove%20istituito

Parotto, E., Lamberti-Castronuovo, A., Censi, V., Valente, M., Atzori, A., & Ragazzoni, L. (2023). Exploring Italian healthcare facilities response to COVID-19 pandemic: Lessons learned from the Italian response to COVID-19 initiative. *Frontiers in Public Health, 10*, 1016649.

Plagg, B., Piccoliori, G., Oschmann, J., Engl, A., & Eisendle, K. (2021). Primary health care and hospital management during COVID-19: Lessons from Lombardy. *Risk Management and Healthcare Policy*, 3987–3992.

Ricci, G., Pallotta, G., Sirignano, A., Amenta, F., & Nittari, G. (2020). Consequences of COVID-19 outbreak in Italy: Medical responsibilities and governmental measures. *Frontiers in Public Health, 8*, 588852.

Ricciardi, W., & Tarricone, R. (2021). The evolution of the Italian national health service. *The Lancet, 398*(10317), 2193–2206.

Romiti, A., Del Vecchio, M., Milani, C., et al. (2023). Italian healthcare organizations facing new dimensions: Changes in governance structure. *Journal of Management and Governance, 27*, 893–921. https://doi.org/10.1007/s10997-021-09618-1

Rotulo, A., Epstein, M., & Kondilis, E. (2020). Fiscal federalism vs fiscal decentralization in healthcare: A conceptual framework. *Hippokratia, 24*(3), 107.

Signorelli, C., Odone, A., Oradini-Alacreu, A., & Pelissero, G. (2020). Universal health coverage in Italy: Lights and shades of the Italian National Health Service which celebrated its 40th anniversary. *Health Policy, 124*(1), 69–74.

Signorelli, C., Pennisi, F., Lunetti, C., Blandi, L., & Pelissero, G. (2024). Quality of hospital care and clinical outcomes: A comparison between the Lombardy region and the Italian national data. *Annali di Igiene, Medicina Preventiva e di Comunità, 36*(2).

Statista. (2024). World's Best Specialized Hospitals 2023 by Newsweek. https://www.newsweek.com/rankings/worlds-best-specialized-hospitals-2023/neurology

Tanese, A. (2023). A new challenge for Italy's national healthcare system. Hospital. *Administration and Medical Practices, 2*.

Tarricone, R., Amatucci, F., Armeni, P., Banks, H., Borsoi, L., Callea, G., Ciani, O., Costa, F., Federici, C., Torbica, A., & Marletta, M. (2021). Establishing a national HTA program for medical devices in Italy: Overhauling a fragmented system to ensure value and equal access to new medical technologies. *Health Policy, 125*(5), 602–608.

Tehrani, N., & Meckl-Sloan, C. (2016). Patient engagement meets personalized interactive communication and the 3P's: Patients, providers and payers. *International Journal of Scientific and Research Publications, 6*(5).

Torbica, A., & Fattore, G. (2005). The "essential levels of care" in Italy: When being explicit serves the devolution of powers. *The European Journal of Health Economics, 6*, 46–52.

Tousijn, W. (2012). Integrating health and social care: Interprofessional relations of multidisciplinary teams in Italy. *Current Sociology, 60*(4), 522–537. https://doi.org/10.1177/0011392112438335

Tulchinsky, T. H., & Varavikova, E. A. (2014). A history of public health. *The New Public Health, 1*.

Vinh, K. P., Walston, S. L., Szychowski, J., & Hernandez, S. R. (2019). The effect of hospitalists on average length of stay. *Journal of Healthcare Management, 64*(3), 169–184.

Wehling, M. (2021). *Principles of translational science in medicine: From bench to bedside* (3rd ed.). Academic Press.

World Bank Group. (2024). Out-of-pocket expenditure (% of current health expenditure) - Italy. Retrieved on May, 2024, https://data.worldbank.org/indicator/SH.XPD.OOPC.CH.ZS?end=2022&locations=IT&start=2000&view=chart

Chapter 4
Patient Engagement Organizational Strategies

Abstract Patient engagement is the cornerstone of high-quality, patient-centered care, yet implementing it effectively remains a challenge for many healthcare organizations. This chapter examines Fondazione Mondino IRCCS' strategies for enhancing engagement through patient journey mapping, focusing on conditions like Multiple Sclerosis, Parkinson's disease, and headache disorders. Key findings highlight the need for personalized care, multidisciplinary collaboration, and digital innovations like the Mondino Digital Service app. By optimizing front office operations, addressing waiting times, and integrating tailored education into digital tools, Fondazione Mondino IRCCS can improve patient experiences and outcomes. Recommendations include expanding app functionality, fostering digital literacy, and leveraging data for ongoing improvement, offering a model for advancing patient-centered neurological care.

4.1 Introduction

Fondazione Mondino has long recognized the importance of patient engagement in delivering high-quality, patient-centered care. This has become so important that it was included among the strategic lines of the healthcare organization as presented in the previous chapter.

As healthcare systems worldwide shift towards more patient-centric models, the concept of patient engagement has gained significance in both research and practice (Carman et al., 2013). As well-documented and thoroughly explained in the first chapter of this book, patient engagement refers to the active involvement of patients in their own healthcare, encompassing everything from shared decision-making to self-management of chronic conditions (Coulter, 2017; Graffigna & Barello, 2018).

The benefits of effective patient engagement are well-documented in extant literature. Engaged patients tend to have better health outcomes, increased satisfaction with their care, and lower healthcare costs (Hibbard & Greene, 2013). Moreover, patient engagement strategies can lead to improvements in healthcare quality and safety by incorporating patient perspectives and experiences into the care delivery

F. Sanguineti, *The Organizational Impact of Patient Engagement*,
SpringerBriefs in Business, https://doi.org/10.1007/978-3-031-77964-0_4

processes (Prey et al., 2014). But from the point of view of a healthcare organization, where should it start putting these strategies into practice?

To start addressing this question, the current chapter provides an overview of the general patient journey at Fondazione Mondino and then focuses on reporting the journey of patients with three of the most common neurological disorders in Italy identified in headache disorders, Parkinson's disease, and multiple sclerosis. The analysis of these patient journeys helped in identifying differences as well as commonalities across the various journeys. The common touchpoints across the various journeys could be seen as the starting points for Fondazione Mondino to begin engaging patients at the organization level.

Thus, this chapter examines the patient engagement strategies employed at Fondazione Mondino, with a particular focus on the first touchpoints the patient has with the organization. By analyzing both qualitative and quantitative data, we aim to identify experienced challenges, developed best practices, and available opportunities for enhancing patient engagement at the organizational level.

4.2 Patient Journey at Fondazione Mondino IRCCS

Patient journey mapping is a powerful tool for understanding and improving the patient experience in healthcare settings (McCarthy et al., 2016). It provides a visual representation of the patients' experience throughout their interactions with the healthcare system, highlighting key touchpoints, pain points, and opportunities for engagement (Trebble et al., 2010). Such a tool pushes healthcare organizations to identify all the points of interactions with a patient, from the initial contact to the posttreatment follow-up (McCarthy et al., 2016). By mapping the whole journey of the patient, healthcare organizations have the chance to identify also opportunities for improvements that would otherwise probably remain unnoticed (Crosier & Handford, 2012). Furthermore, it allows healthcare organizations to step into the patient's shoes and see the healthcare system from their perspective. Thus, the importance of mapping the patient journey is reflected in its ability to provide a proper understanding of the patient experience (Bitner et al., 2008). This understanding is crucial for identifying areas where, for example, patient engagement can be enhanced.

We have decided to focus on the patient journey at Fondazione Mondino as it can be particularly useful for several reasons: First, mapping out the patient journey helps in identifying the touchpoints where patients interact with the organization (Trebble et al., 2010). These contact points, if properly addressed, offer opportunities for improving patient's experiences. Second, the patient journey map can help in distinguishing between the interaction points that are more correctly under the responsibility of the organization and those that are, instead, better off under the responsibility of the head of the department, for example. This distinction may help in developing specific engagement strategies and assigning accountability for their implementation. Third, it can support identifying areas where resources need to be allocated to support patient engagement initiatives. By highlighting the various touchpoints and the specific needs of patients at each step of their journey (Trebble et al., 2010), healthcare organizations can make informed decisions about where and how to invest for improving and enhancing patient engagement strategies.

This patient journey mapping approach is particularly important in complex healthcare environments such as Fondazione Mondino, where patients often have to deal with various departments and services over extended periods of time. Figure 4.1 graphically summarizes the general patient journey at Fondazione Mondino.

As depicted in Fig. 4.1, the patient journey at Fondazione Mondino involves nine main touchpoints. Specifically:

1. Initial contact. This may occur through various channels, including referrals from primary care physicians, emergency visits, or self-referrals. The quality of information provided at this stage can significantly impact the patient's perception and preparation for subsequent interactions.
2. Appointment scheduling. This step involves the patient's first direct interaction with Fondazione Mondino's systems, often through the Central Unified Booking (*Centro Unico Prenotazioni*—CUP) system, the call center and back office of the Fondazione Mondino, or, increasingly, through digital platforms like the recently launched Mondino digital service app.
3. Pre-visit information gathering. Patients often seek information about their condition and the upcoming visit. Fondazione Mondino's ability to provide clear, accessible information at this stage can greatly enhance patient preparation and reduce anxiety.
4. Check-in. The physical environment and the efficiency of the check-in process play a crucial role in setting the tone for the patient's next steps. This includes interactions with front office staff, easy access to the facility, and acceptable waiting times.
5. Clinical visit. This core interaction with healthcare providers is critical for patient satisfaction and engagement. It includes not only the medical aspects but also the quality of communication and the degree of shared decision-making. The more the clinician and the care team empathize with the patient, the better the outcome will be.
6. Diagnostic testing. For many neurological conditions, this may involve complex or unfamiliar procedures. Clear explanation and supportive staff can significantly improve the patient experience during these processes.
7. Treatment planning. This step is crucial for patient engagement, involving discussions about treatment options, potential outcomes, and patient preferences. In this step, the care team must evaluate the patient's point of view carefully. It is of utmost importance that the treatment is aligned with patient's lifestyle and expectations.
8. Follow-up care and ongoing management. For chronic neurological conditions, this touchpoint is particularly important, involving regular check-ups, medication management, and, often, lifestyle changes. The main objective of most healthcare professionals is to reduce lifestyle modifications as much as possible,

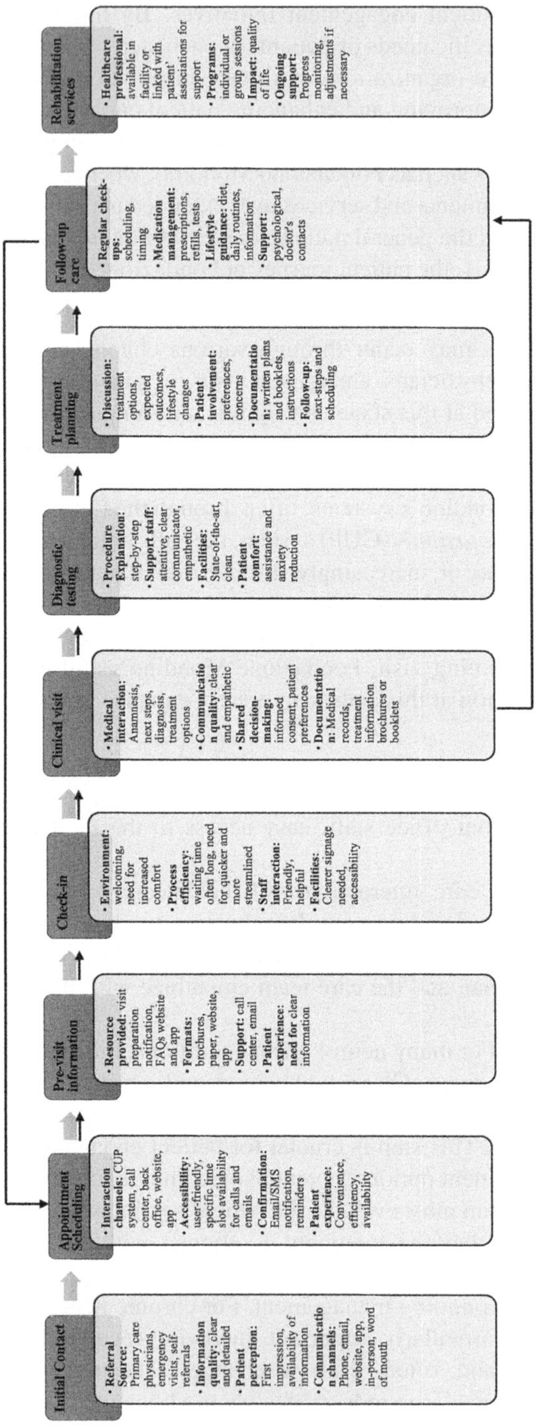

Fig. 4.1 Patient journey at Fondazione Mondino. *Source*: own elaboration

so that patients, even with a chronic neurological disease, can live their lives in the best possible way.

9. Rehabilitation services. When applicable, this step involves ongoing interactions with various healthcare professionals that can significantly—positively—impact the patient's quality of life and functional outcomes.

Therefore, mapping the patient journey at Fondazione Mondino captures the key touchpoints that patients typically experience when interacting with the healthcare organization. It is important to note that while this journey is presented mostly linearly, in reality, especially for patients with chronic neurological conditions, many of these touchpoints will be revisited multiple times throughout the course of their patient journey. For example, appointment scheduling is not a one-time event, but rather a recurring touchpoint. After initial treatment planning, patients will need to schedule follow-up appointments for ongoing care.

Furthermore, the journey mapping process reveals that certain touchpoints, such as initial contact, appointment scheduling, and check-in, are more closely tied to organizational-level operations. These touchpoints are often managed by front office staff and central booking systems, and the efficiency and quality of these interactions can significantly impact the overall patient experience.

In contrast, touchpoints like clinical visits, diagnostic testing, and treatment planning are more disease-specific and require more specialized approaches depending on the patient's condition. These touchpoints should be kept under the responsibility of individual departments or healthcare professionals, who can leverage their expertise to provide personalized care and improve engagement strategies.

By recognizing the distinct nature of these touchpoints, Fondazione Mondino can develop a multi-level approach to patient engagement. At the organizational level, efforts might focus on streamlining processes, enhancing communication, and improving the overall patient experience across all departments. At the department or disease-specific level, targeted interventions can be implemented to address the unique needs and challenges of each patient population.

Nevertheless, each of these touchpoints presents unique opportunities for patient engagement and experience enhancement. By mapping these journeys on regular basis, Fondazione Mondino can identify critical moments where interventions can most effectively improve patient outcomes and satisfaction.

For example, the journey mapping at Fondazione Mondino has revealed that while clinical care is generally highly regarded, there are opportunities to enhance the patient experience in areas such as appointment scheduling, waiting times, and information provision. These insights have led to targeted improvements, including the introduction of digital solutions like the Mondino Digital Service app.

4.3 Focus on Some Specific Patient Journeys

While the general patient journey at Fondazione Mondino provides a broad overview of the patient experience, it is important to also take a deeper look into some of the specific journeys of patients with different neurological conditions. One of the findings from the previous section of this chapter is that while patient journeys are specific to each disease and should be developed and adapted accordingly, there are some common touchpoints that Fondazione Mondino could impact while leaving those specifics to the disease in the hands of the Head of each department. Therefore, this section delves into the unique experiences of patients with multiple sclerosis (MS), Parkinson's disease (PD), and headache disorders to identify which touchpoints should be left to the responsibility of each department and in which interaction points would instead make sense for Fondazione Mondino to intervene.

The selection of these specific disorders—multiple sclerosis (MS), Parkinson's disease (PD), and headache disorders—was based on several factors. First of all, MS, PD, and headache are among the most common neurological conditions in Italy, affecting millions of individuals and placing a substantial burden on the healthcare system (i.e., Paz-Zulueta et al., 2020). As a matter of fact, MS patients in Italy are approximately 133,000, with an estimated increase of about 3600 new cases each year (Bandiera et al., 2022). PD patients are estimated to be around 300,000 (Osservatorio Malattie Rare, 2023), while a great portion of the Italian population suffers from headache (Allena et al., 2015). Their chronic nature requires long-term management and ongoing patient engagement, making them ideal for studying the full spectrum of the patient journey. Moreover, each condition affects a different demographic profile, allowing for a comprehensive analysis of engagement strategies across various age groups and life stages. Also, these disorders often require multidisciplinary care approaches, providing insights into the challenges of coordinating complex treatment plans. All three conditions are also active areas of clinical research, allowing for the examination of patient engagement in the context of clinical trials.

To gather data on these specific patient journeys, we employed a mixed-methods approach. We conducted semi-structured interviews with key informants at Fondazione Mondino, including Heads of departments and Specialists in MS, PD, and headache disorders. These interviews, lasting an average of 50 min each, provided rich, qualitative data on patient experiences, challenges, and current engagement strategies. Based on the interview data and additional patient insights, we created detailed patient personas for each condition, representing typical patient profiles encountered at Fondazione Mondino.

Drawing from the collected data, we propose visual representations of the patient journeys for each disease, highlighting key touchpoints, challenges, and opportunities for enhanced engagement. By examining these specific journeys in detail, we aim to identify both common themes and condition-specific nuances that can inform more targeted and effective patient engagement strategies at the department level while highlighting which interaction points are of utmost importance at the organization level. In other words, which are the specific steps Fondazione Mondino should begin targeting to enhance patient engagement while improving organizational process efficiency?

In the following subsections, we report our findings for each condition, including detailed patient journeys and identified patient persona, followed by a comparative analysis that synthesizes key insights for enhancing overall patient engagement.

Through this in-depth exploration, we seek to uncover some of the patient experiences within Fondazione Mondino, revealing the unique challenges and opportunities each department faces. At the same time, the analysis will highlight common touchpoints on which the IRCCS should focus to actively implement patient engagement strategies, thus putting into practice one of its defined strategic lines—as introduced in the previous chapter.

4.3.1 Multiple Sclerosis

Multiple sclerosis is an autoimmune disease that profoundly affects the central nervous system and that can have a significant impact on patients' quality of life. It is characterized by inflammation and damage to the myelin, the protective sheath surrounding nerve fibers (Hauser & Cree, 2020). This damage leads to problematic communication between the brain and the rest of the body, causing a wide range of symptoms, including motor problems, balance difficulties, fatigue, and cognitive impairments (Lakin et al., 2021). The progression of the disease is variable and can include episodes of relapses and remissions or a continuous decline (Inojosa et al., 2020).

In Italy, MS affects approximately 133,000 individuals, with a notably higher incidence among young adults and women (Bandiera et al., 2022). This prevalence underscores the importance of understanding and optimizing the patient journey for those affected by MS. Managing the disease itself represents a significant challenge for the Italian healthcare system. Early diagnosis and timely treatment are crucial for slowing the progression of the disease and improving patients' quality of life (Blaschke et al., 2022). Treatment options include disease-modifying therapies, such as immunomodulators and immunosuppressants, and symptomatic treatments to alleviate specific symptoms (Hauser & Cree, 2020). Additionally, multidisciplinary care involving neurologists, physiotherapists, occupational therapists, psychologists, and other specialists is essential for providing comprehensive support to patients (Van Hijfte et al., 2024).

The role of patient associations is crucial in the context of multiple sclerosis in Italy. Organizations like AISM (Italian Multiple Sclerosis Association) provide support, information, and advocacy, contributing to improving the quality of life for people affected by MS. These associations offer assistance programs, psychological support, and promote research for new therapies (e.g., Bezzini et al., 2020).

The Italian healthcare system, despite economic and organizational challenges, continues to provide substantial support to patients with multiple sclerosis. Integrated care networks and specialized centers offer high-quality services, and continuous training of healthcare professionals is essential to ensure that care aligns with the latest scientific evidence.

Fondazione Mondino is one of the leading institutions in MS care. Here, the patient journey for MS is characterized by several key stages, as illustrated in Fig. 4.2. Again, the patient journey begins with the onset of initial symptoms and

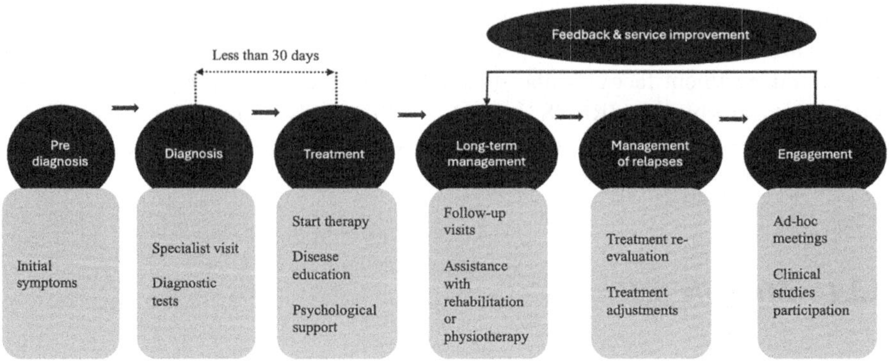

Fig. 4.2 Multiple sclerosis patient journey at Fondazione Mondino. *Source:* own elaboration

progresses through diagnosis, treatment initiation, follow-up care which includes diagnostic tests run on regular basis, and potential participation in clinical trials.

The journey starts with patients experiencing their first symptoms, often leading to consultations with general practitioners or emergency visits. This initial phase is crucial, as timely referral to neurological specialists can significantly impact the course of the disease (Blaschke et al., 2022). Then, individuals often ask for referrals to where to go for potential diagnosis and care—they might ask their physicians, friends, and family—or even look for suggestions online. Upon reaching Fondazione Mondino, patients undergo comprehensive diagnostic procedures, including MRI scans and lumbar punctures, to confirm the MS diagnosis. At Fondazione Mondino, the time between the onset of the symptoms—or the moment in which the individuals enter the hospital facility looking for a diagnosis—and the diagnosis of MS takes, on average, less than 30 days.

Following diagnosis, patients enter a phase of treatment initiation and education. This stage is particularly critical for patient engagement, as it involves shared decision-making regarding treatment options and lifestyle changes. Fondazione Mondino places a strong emphasis on patient education during this phase, equipping not only individuals but also their caregivers with the knowledge and tools to actively participate and support in the healthcare journey.

The ongoing management phase represents the longest and most variable part of the patient journey. It encompasses regular follow-up appointments, monitoring of disease progression and potential relapsing phases, and adjustments to treatment plans as needed. During this phase, the department at Fondazione Mondino dedicated to MS leverages multidisciplinary care teams, including neurologists, nurses, physiotherapists, and psychologists, to address the diverse needs of MS patients.

For some patients, the journey may include participation in clinical trials, offering access to innovative treatments and contributing to the advancement of MS research. Fondazione Mondino's strong research focus provides patients with opportunities to engage in cutting-edge studies, with the hope to support and facilitate their patient experience.

The main identified challenge is the contact between patient and the care team, which the department dedicated to MS has addressed by offering a dedicated nurse or research secretary that responds to potential doubts or frequently asked questions from patients. All these raised questions that the front office is not equipped to handle is, therefore, managed by members of the care team itself.

While investigating the MS' patient journey, our study revealed that there are two main patient personas that encapsulate the diverse experiences of individuals with MS treated at Fondazione Mondino. Identifying patient personas is an important step in properly understanding the various experiences of patients. A patient persona is a semi-fictional character that represents a specific segment of the patient population, developed on the bases of demographic and psychographic characteristics, together with behavioral patterns (Harley, 2015; LeRouge et al., 2013). By creating detailed profiles of these personas, healthcare organizations can gain insights on how to improve the service provided.

Thus, the identification of these personas, as depicted in Fig. 4.3, aims at providing insights regarding the needs and challenges faced by MS patients.

The first persona represents a young adult, typically female and between 25 and 35 years old. This individual is often well-educated and technologically savvy and actively seeks information about their condition. Their biggest challenge is balancing their career aspirations and personal life with the unpredictable nature of

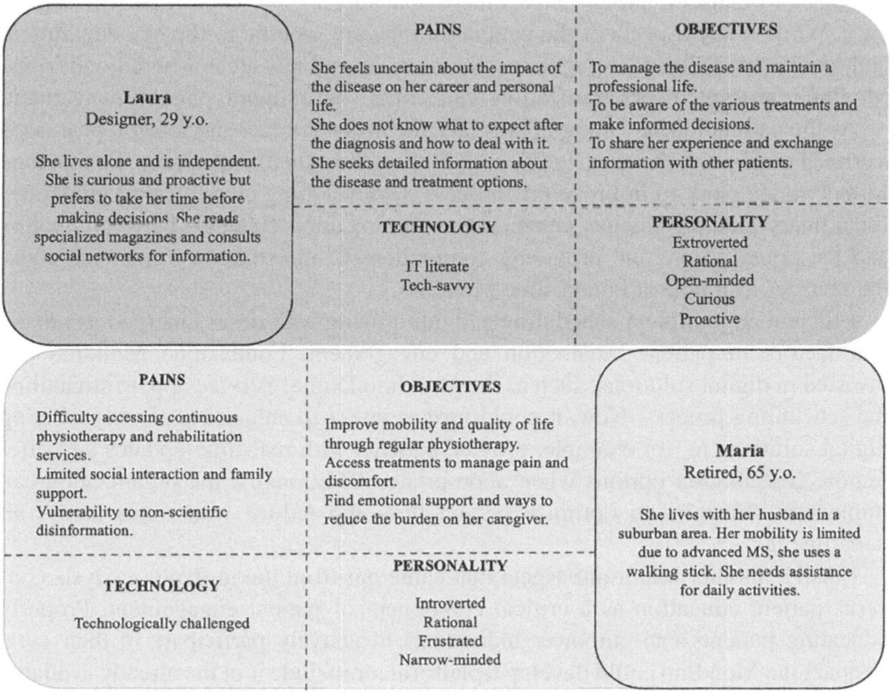

Fig. 4.3 Multiple sclerosis patient personas at Fondazione Mondino. *Source:* own elaboration

MS. These patients value digital engagement tools, comprehensive information resources, and flexible care options that can fit with their active lifestyles.

In contrast, the second persona depicts a middle-aged adult with advanced disability, usually between 50 and 65 years old. This individual often faces significant physical limitations and may have experienced a reduction in work capacity due to MS progression. They rely more heavily on family support and have a more complex relationship with healthcare services. These patients prioritize accessibility, comprehensive support services, and interventions aimed at maintaining a good quality of life and independence.

Therefore, the identification of these personas provides valuable insights on how healthcare services could be tailored to patients' needs, thus enhancing patient engagement and overall experience.

Recommendations at Organizational Level for Enhancing Patient Engagement in MS

The identification of patient journey and the development of patient personas offer insights that provide the basis for recommendations to address the diverse needs and challenges faced by MS patients at Fondazione Mondino. By understanding the unique experiences of these patient segments, the organization can develop targeted strategies to enhance patient engagement and improve the overall patient experience. While many aspects of the patient journey are specific to the MS department and require specialized interventions, there are several key areas where Fondazione Mondino can implement organization-wide initiatives to support patient engagement.

As the patient journey mapping reveals, the initial contact and referral process is a critical touchpoint that can significantly impact the patient experience. Fondazione Mondino can work to improve this process by developing clear referral guidelines for primary care physicians, enhancing communication channels between doctors and the organization, and providing comprehensive information to patients about the services available at Fondazione Mondino.

Efficient appointment scheduling and minimizing wait times emerged as important factors in patient satisfaction and engagement. Fondazione Mondino has invested in digital solutions, such as the Mondino Digital Service app, to streamline the scheduling process. Now, it could further invest in enhancing already existing digital solutions to, for example, provide patients with real-time updates and offer remote consultation options when appropriate. Additionally, the organization can implement strategies to optimize patient flow and reduce wait times across all departments.

Finally, another important aspect that came out from the in-depth analysis concerns patient education as a critical component of patient engagement. Properly educating patients can empower individuals to actively participate in their care. Fondazione Mondino could develop a platform, or include it in the already available ones, that each department should then integrate with information that cater to the needs of different patient personas. These resources should cover topics such as disease management, treatment options, lifestyle modifications, and available support services.

Therefore, while the MS patient journey and personas highlight the importance of specialized, department-level interventions, they also reveal key opportunities for Fondazione Mondino to enhance patient engagement at the organizational level. As a matter of fact, thanks to the highlighted areas of improvement, the organization can create a strong foundation for patient engagement that benefits all patients, regardless of their specific neurological condition.

4.3.2 Parkinson's Disease

Parkinson's disease (PD) is as a chronic, progressive neurodegenerative disorder that affects the central nervous system, thus impacting movement, balance, and coordination (Poewe et al., 2017). Additionally, patients may experience nonmotor symptoms such as sleep disorders, depression, anxiety, cognitive impairment, and gastrointestinal issues (Schapira et al., 2017). These symptoms can significantly impact patients' quality of life and independence.

In Italy, it is estimated that approximately 300,000 individuals are affected by PD, with an increasing prevalence in the aging population, but it more and more affects even younger adults (Istituto Superiore di Sanità, 2018; Riccò et al., 2020; Vanacore & Morgante, 2001). Each year, around 6000 new cases are diagnosed, with a higher incidence in men compared to women. Parkinson's disease represents a significant burden on the national healthcare system, with high direct costs (medical care, medications, hospitalization) and indirect costs (productivity loss, long-term care) (Chaudhuri et al., 2024; Riccò et al., 2020).

Italy is actively involved in Parkinson's research, with numerous clinical studies and specialized centers dedicated to improving the understanding and management of the disease (Riccò et al., 2020). Despite the availability of various pharmacological and surgical treatments, such as levodopa and deep brain stimulation, there remains a significant unmet need for more effective and personalized therapeutic approaches (Antonini et al., 2018). Early diagnosis, multidisciplinary care, and patient engagement are crucial factors in optimizing patient outcomes and quality of life (Bloem et al., 2020; Riccò et al., 2020).

This growing impact underscores the critical importance of understanding and optimizing the patient journey for those affected by PD. Being Fondazione Mondino a recognized leading center for Parkinson's disease treatment, with the most advanced cure and active clinical trials, investigating the most important touchpoints between the organization and the patients can provide insights for a continuous improvement while highlighting the best practices already in place.

Thus, Fig. 4.4 depicts the patient journey for Parkinson's disease at Fondazione Mondino. It is marked by several distinct phases, each presenting unique challenges and opportunities for patient engagement.

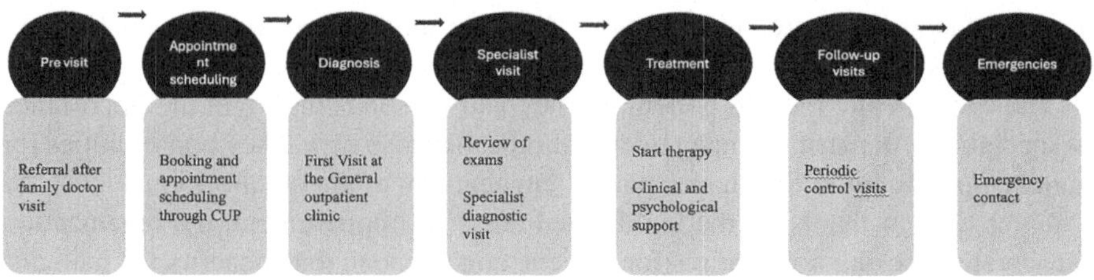

Fig. 4.4 Parkinson's disease patient journey at Fondazione Mondino. *Source:* own elaboration

This journey begins with the onset of early symptoms, often leading to initial consultations with general practitioners. As symptoms become more pronounced, patients are referred to neurological specialists for comprehensive evaluation and diagnosis. Patients usually arrive at Fondazione Mondino because of its renowned experience and treatments, after the referral from friends, family, or doctors or after having surfed the internet for center of reference for neurological diseases. Once they decide for Fondazione Mondino, they make the appointment and then physically visit the hospital facility.

The diagnostic phase involves a series of specialized assessments, including neurological examinations, imaging studies, and, in some cases, genetic testing. This phase is crucial not only for confirming the diagnosis but also for establishing a baseline for future disease progression monitoring. The diagnosis represents a critical moment in the patient journey, often accompanied by a range of emotions and the need for immediate support and education.

Following diagnosis, patients enter a phase of treatment initiation and adjustment. This stage involves collaborative decision-making between patients and their care team regarding treatment options, which may include dopaminergic medications, physical therapy, and lifestyle changes. The Parkinson's department at Fondazione Mondino places significant emphasis on patient education during this phase, empowering individuals and their caregivers with knowledge about their condition and treatment options.

The ongoing management phase constitutes the longest and most variable part of the PD patient journey, being it a chronic and progressive disease. It encompasses regular follow-up appointments, treatment adjustments, and the management of both motor and nonmotor symptoms. During this phase, the department leverages a multidisciplinary approach, involving neurologists, nurses, physiotherapists, speech therapists, and psychologists to address the diverse and evolving needs of PD patients.

For patients with advanced PD, the journey may include consideration of advanced therapies such as deep brain stimulation or continuous dopaminergic infusion therapies. The department expertise in these advanced treatments provides patients with access to cutting-edge care options when standard therapies become less effective. Also, throughout the journey, patients have the opportunity to participate in clinical trials, contributing to the advancement of PD research while accessing innovative treatments. Fondazione Mondino's strong research focus enhances this aspect of the patient journey, offering the possibility for novel therapeutic approaches.

The main identified challenge is the contact between patient and the care team, which would benefit from a dedicated nurse or research secretary—as is the case for MS—that addresses potential doubts or frequently asked questions from patients that the front office is not equipped to handle or respond to.

Following the same approach applied when investigating multiple sclerosis at Fondazione Mondino, while investigating the patients journey of PD, our study revealed two main patient personas that represent the diverse experiences of individuals with Parkinson's disease treated at the dedicated department. As in the MS' case, these personas, depicted in Fig. 4.5, offer insights into the varied needs and challenges faced by PD patients at different stages of their journey.

The first persona represents a newly diagnosed patient, typically around 35 years old. This individual is often still actively engaged in their career and striving to maintain an active lifestyle. They face the challenge of adapting to their diagnosis while balancing work responsibilities and personal life. These patients value early intervention strategies, flexible treatment options that accommodate their work schedules, and resources to help them navigate the initial stages of living with PD, reducing the associated anxiety.

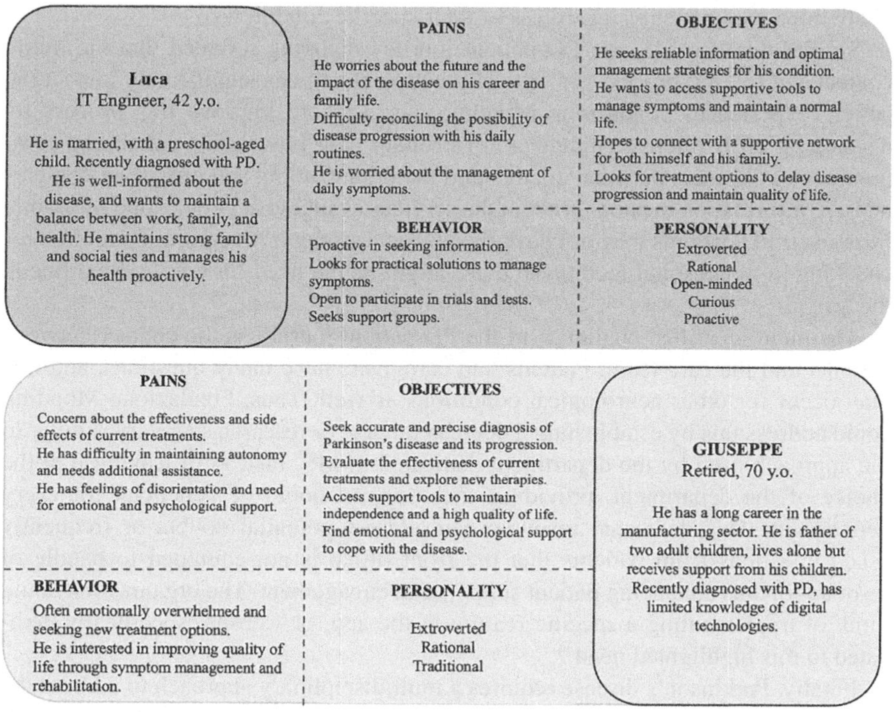

Fig. 4.5 Parkinson's disease patient personas at Fondazione Mondino. *Source:* own elaboration

In contrast, the second persona depicts a patient in an advanced stage of PD, usually around 72 years old. This individual is typically retired and facing significant mobility challenges. They often rely heavily on caregiver support for daily activities. These patients prioritize comprehensive symptom management, accessibility of care services, and interventions aimed at maintaining quality of life and independence. They also value support services for their caregivers, recognizing the significant role family members play in their care.

Recommendations at Organizational Level for Enhancing Patient Engagement in PD

As for the case of MS, also, the identification of PD patient journey and patient personas provides interesting insights into the diverse needs and challenges faced by individuals with a particular disease, Parkinson's, at Fondazione Mondino. By understanding the unique experiences of these patient segments, the organization can develop targeted strategies to enhance patient engagement and improve the overall patient experience.

Again, while many aspects of the patient journey are peculiar to the disease and should remain under the responsibility of the experts' team, there are areas in which Fondazione Mondino could implement organization-wide initiatives that will positively impact all patients, regardless of their specific condition.

Similar than for MS, the PD patient journey mapping revealed that the initial contact and referral process is a critical touchpoint that can significantly impact the patient experience. Fondazione Mondino can work to improve this process by developing clear referral guidelines for primary care physicians, enhancing communication channels between doctors and the organization, and providing comprehensive information to patients about the services available at Fondazione Mondino. Moreover, PD patients may not have the physical strength for waiting long time for checking in the hospital facility, so there might be the need for a prioritized line at the arrival.

The main identified challenge in the PD patient journey is the contact between patients and the care team. Patients and caregivers have many questions, and this may occur for other neurological conditions as well. Thus, Fondazione Mondino could address this by establishing a dedicated nurse or research secretary, similar to the approach used by the department dedicated to MS. Instead of leaving it at the choice of the department, providing such support could be beneficial for every department. This dedicated resource can address potential doubts or frequently asked questions from patients that the front office is not equipped to handle or respond to, thus enhancing patient support and engagement. The organization could think of implementing a specific feature in the app, or website, specifically dedicated to this highlighted need.

Finally, Parkinson's disease requires a multidisciplinary approach to address the diverse and evolving needs of patients. Fondazione Mondino can encourage collaboration among various departments to provide comprehensive care for their patients. By promoting a multidisciplinary approach across the organization, Fondazione Mondino can ensure that patients receive the actually needed support throughout the whole journey.

By addressing these key areas at the organizational level, Fondazione Mondino can create a foundation for effective patient engagement that complements the specialized interventions implemented within the PD department.

4.3.3 Headache Disorders

Headache disorders, encompassing a wide spectrum of conditions including migraines, tension-type headaches, and cluster headaches, represent a significant burden on patients' quality of life and the healthcare system (Steiner et al., 2019). These disorders are characterized by pain or discomfort in the head or neck region and are among the most prevalent and debilitating neurological conditions (Stovner et al., 2018). In Italy, headache disorders are classified into two main categories: primary headaches and secondary headaches. Primary headaches include migraine, tension-type headache, and cluster headache (Barbanti, 2019).

Migraine is characterized by recurrent attacks of throbbing pain, often accompanied by nausea, vomiting, and sensitivity to light and sound (Goadsby et al., 2017). Tension-type headache is the most common form of headache, with diffuse, mild to moderate intensity pain (Bendtsen et al., 2016). Cluster headache, while rare, is extremely painful, with short, intense attacks occurring in series. Secondary headaches, on the other hand, are symptoms of underlying medical conditions such as infections, head trauma, vascular disorders, or metabolic issues (Sacco et al., 2020). Diagnosing secondary headaches requires careful medical evaluation to identify and treat the primary cause of the pain (Barbanti, 2019).

In Italy, the treatment of headache disorders presents a significant challenge for the healthcare system. According to data from the Istituto Superiore di Sanità, millions of Italians suffer from chronic headaches, with a substantial impact on work productivity and quality of life (Allena et al., 2015). Headache disorders are among the leading causes of absenteeism and reduced work efficiency, contributing to a significant economic burden for both patients and society (Martelletti et al., 2018).

The treatment of headache disorders in Italy is based on a multidisciplinary approach that includes pharmacological management, behavioral therapy, and preventive interventions (Barbanti, 2019). Medications used to treat headaches include analgesics, nonsteroidal anti-inflammatory drugs, triptans for migraine, and preventive drugs to reduce the frequency and severity of attacks (Sarchielli et al., 2012).

Despite advances in understanding and treating headache disorders, many people continue to suffer significantly. Public awareness and education of healthcare professionals are essential for improving the diagnosis and management of headache disorders (Steiner et al., 2019). Research initiatives continue to explore new therapies and preventive strategies to alleviate the burden of this pervasive and debilitating condition (Tassorelli et al., 2021).

The pervasive nature of headache disorders underscores the importance of a specialized approach to patient care and engagement. Being Fondazione Mondino a leading center for headache treatment, examining the patient journey can significantly help in identifying best practices and touchpoints to address for an always improved patient experience.

Thus, the patient journey for headache disorders at the dedicated department at Fondazione Mondino, as illustrated in Fig. 4.6, is characterized by a series of distinct phases, each presenting unique challenges and opportunities for patient engagement as for the previous two investigated diseases.

This journey begins with patients experiencing recurrent or severe headaches that significantly impact their daily lives. Many individuals initially seek help from their general practitioners or attempt self-management with over-the-counter medications. As the condition persists or worsens, they are typically referred to a specialized headache center. Therefore, individuals often seek suggestions from friends and family, doctors, or online. They often come to Fondazione Mondino due to its renowned experience as well as state-of-the-art treatments. Once having decided for this organization, they make the appointment for a first-time visit.

Upon entering the care pathway at Fondazione Mondino, patients undergo a comprehensive initial consultation. This crucial touchpoint involves patient's anamnesis, physical examinations, and, when necessary, specialized diagnostic tests. The diagnostic phase is particularly important for differentiating between various types of headache disorders and identifying any underlying causes. Fondazione Mondino's expertise in neurological conditions allows for precise diagnosis, setting the foundation for effective treatment planning.

Following diagnosis, patients enter a phase of treatment initiation and education. This stage is critical for patient engagement, as it involves collaborative decision-making regarding treatment options. For migraine patients, this may include preventive medications, acute treatments, and lifestyle modifications. Cluster headache patients, given the severity of their condition, often require more aggressive interventions. Fondazione Mondino places significant emphasis on patient education during this phase, empowering individuals with knowledge about their specific headache disorder, trigger factors, and management strategies.

The ongoing management phase constitutes a significant portion of the patient journey also for headache patients. It involves regular follow-up appointments,

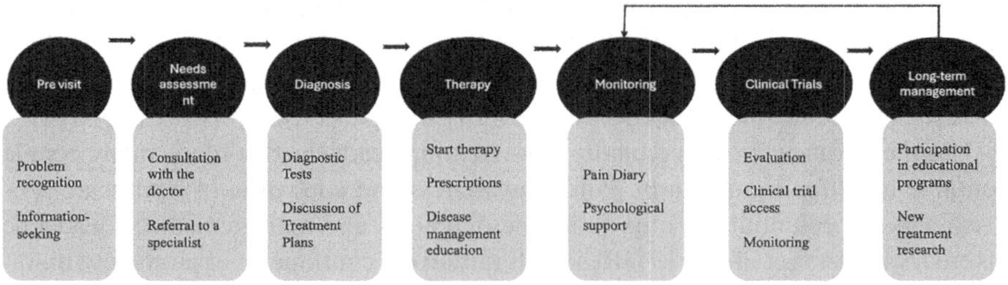

Fig. 4.6 Headache disease patient journey at Fondazione Mondino. *Source:* own elaboration

treatment adjustments, and the implementation of non-pharmacological interventions.

For patients with refractory headaches, the journey may include access to innovative treatments such as neurostimulation techniques or participation in clinical trials. Once again, Fondazione Mondino's commitment to research in headache disorders provides patients with opportunities to benefit from cutting-edge therapies and contribute to advancements in the field.

Following the same approach applied for the other two investigated diseases, our research identified two main patient personas that encapsulate the diverse experiences of individuals with headache disorders treated by the dedicated department at Fondazione Mondino. As previously highlighted, recognizing these personas—now depicted in Fig. 4.7—offer insights into the various needs and challenges faced by patients with different types of headache disorders.

The first persona represents a typical migraine patient, often a woman around 38 years old. This individual often takes care of work and family responsibilities while managing recurrent, debilitating migraine attacks. She values flexible treatment options that can be integrated into her busy lifestyle, rapid relief for acute attacks, and strategies to prevent migraines from disrupting her professional and personal life. This patient is often well-informed about her condition but seeks expert guidance to optimize her disease management strategy.

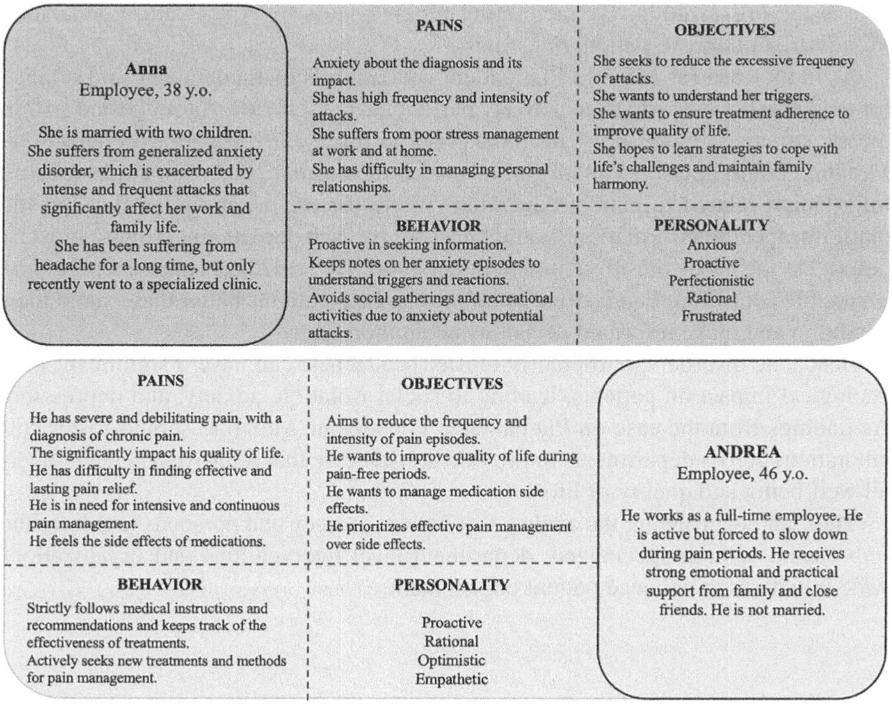

Fig. 4.7 Headache disorder patient personas at Fondazione Mondino. *Source:* own elaboration

The second persona depicts a cluster headache patient, typically a man around 46 years old. This person faces extremely severe pain episodes that significantly impact his daily life and work capacity. The intensity and unpredictability of cluster headache attacks often lead to social isolation and psychological distress. This patient prioritizes rapid and effective pain relief, access to specialized care during acute episodes, and comprehensive support to manage the psychological impact of the condition.

Recommendations at Organizational Level for Enhancing Patient Engagement in PD

As in the case for MS and PD, the identification of headache disease's patient journey and patient personas helped in highlighting aspects that are specific to the disease management while also recognizing potential organization-level interventions that might enhance patient engagement at Fondazione Mondino overall.

As the headache disorder patient journey mapping reveals, many individuals initially seek help from general practitioners or attempt self-management before being referred to a specialized headache center. Fondazione Mondino can work to streamline the referral process by collaborating with primary care providers, developing clear referral guidelines, and raising awareness about the specialized services available at the organization. By facilitating timely access to expert care, Fondazione Mondino can improve patient outcomes.

As in the case for MS and PD, patient education is of fundamental importance for empowering individuals to actively participate in their care. As suggested within the recommendation resulting from the previous disease investigations, Fondazione Mondino could develop a platform, or enrich the current ones, to include specific information related to patient education. While the organization can develop the platform, specific information should be added by each department as these must be tailored to the needs of different patient personas. By providing comprehensive and accessible education, Fondazione Mondino can help patients better understand their condition and make informed decisions about their care.

Headache disorders, particularly cluster headaches, can have a significant psychological impact on patients, leading to social isolation, anxiety, and depression. As findings from the case on PD patients, Fondazione Mondino should foster collaborations across departments to provide holistic care that improves patients' overall well-being and quality of life.

Thus, and once again, the analyses of patient journey and personas highlight the importance of both specialized, department-level interventions and organization-wide initiatives to enhance patient engagement.

4.3.4 Comparative Analysis and Implications for Patient Engagement

The in-depth exploration of patient journeys for general neurological patients and specific multiple sclerosis, Parkinson's disease, and headache disorder patients revealed a complex mix of experiences, challenges, and opportunities for patient engagement.

A striking commonality across all the analyses is the critical role of the initial contact and referral process. This touchpoint serves as the entry point for patients seeking specialized care at Fondazione Mondino and can significantly impact their overall experience and outcomes. Across all three examined conditions, the organization has an opportunity to streamline and optimize this process to ensure patients receive timely access to appropriate care and support.

To improve the initial contact and referral process, Fondazione Mondino should focus on developing clear referral guidelines for primary care physicians and other healthcare providers. These guidelines should outline the specific criteria for referring patients with suspected neurological disorders to the specialized departments at the organization. By providing clear guidance, Fondazione Mondino can help ensure that patients are referred promptly and appropriately, reducing delays in diagnosis and treatment initiation. Additionally, the organization should enhance communication channels between referring physicians and the specialized departments, facilitating information exchange and collaboration. This can involve establishing dedicated referral coordinators, implementing secure messaging systems, or creating online referral portals. By encouraging and fostering open and efficient communication, Fondazione Mondino can streamline the referral process and ensure continuity of care for patients transitioning from primary care to specialized services.

Furthermore, Fondazione Mondino should prioritize providing comprehensive information to patients about the available services and what to expect during their care journey. This can involve developing patient-friendly materials, such as brochures, videos, or online resources, that clearly explain the specialized services offered for each specific disorder. These materials should cover topics such as the expertise of the clinical teams, diagnostic procedures, treatment options, and support services available. By proactively educating patients about the care they will receive at Fondazione Mondino, the organization can alleviate anxiety, set realistic expectations, and empower patients to actively participate in their healthcare decisions. Moreover, for patients with mobility limitations, the organization should consider implementing accommodations like prioritized check-in lines or expedited registration processes to minimize waiting times. By providing targeted information and support from the initial contact point, Fondazione Mondino can create a positive and patient-centered experience from the very beginning of the journey.

Another important outcome is the identification of back and front office as one of the initial touchpoints in the patient journey. This finding underscores the necessity for Fondazione Mondino to address front office operations as a foundational element of patient engagement. The front office serves as the gateway to the institution, shaping first impressions and setting the tone for the entire care experience. It represents a unique opportunity for the organization to establish an efficient entry point for all patients, regardless of their specific neurological condition.

Beyond the front office, the responsibility for patient engagement naturally shifts to the specific departments and their respective heads. This transition reflects the increasing specialization of care as patients progress through their journeys. The comparative analysis reveals that while each neurological condition presents unique challenges, there are several overarching themes in patient engagement that span across departments.

Personalization emerges as a crucial factor in effective patient engagement across all examined conditions. The diverse patient personas identified for MS, Parkinson's, and headache disorders highlight the need for specific care strategies. Department heads play a crucial role in promoting a culture of personalization within their teams, encouraging healthcare providers to tailor their approaches to individual patient needs, preferences, and circumstances, whenever possible. This might involve developing modular education programs, offering multiple treatment pathways, or implementing personalized follow-up protocols.

The long-term nature of the examined neurological conditions necessitates a sustained engagement strategy that evolves with the patient's journey. From the newly diagnosed MS patient grappling with lifestyle adjustments to the advanced Parkinson's patient navigating complex symptom management, the need for continuous support is clear. This longitudinal perspective challenges department heads to develop engagement strategies that remain relevant and effective throughout the patient's life, potentially leveraging technology for ongoing communication and support between clinical visits.

Multidisciplinary care emerges as another common thread across the examined conditions. The complex nature of neurological disorders often requires input from various specialists, therapists, and support services. The challenge lies in coordinating these diverse elements into a cohesive care experience. Fondazione Mondino must encourage interdisciplinary collaboration with the help of Department Heads, for example, through regular case conferences, integrated care plans, or the development of multidisciplinary clinics that bring various specialists together in a single patient visit.

Digital engagement is identified as both an opportunity and a challenge across the examined conditions. The varying levels of digital literacy among patient groups, particularly evident in the contrast between younger MS patients and older Parkinson's patients, underscore the need for a multifaceted approach to digital tools. Department heads and Fondazione Mondino must find a balance between leveraging technology to enhance care delivery and ensuring that less tech-savvy patients are not left behind. This might involve developing hybrid models of care that combine digital and traditional engagement channels.

This comparative analysis reveals that while the front office serves as a crucial, centralized point of initial engagement, the subsequent patient journey mostly requires specialized, department-specific strategies. By addressing front office operations at an organizational level while empowering department heads to tailor engagement strategies to their specific patient populations, Fondazione Mondino can create a comprehensive, nuanced approach to patient engagement that increase patient engagement across all neurological conditions. Thus, one area that has emerged as particularly crucial in shaping the overall patient experience, and that can be indeed targeted by the management of Fondazione Mondino without having to engage each department, is the front office interaction. As the first point of contact for many patients, the efficiency and quality of these interactions can set the tone for the entire patient journey. Therefore, a closer examination of front office operations is warranted to understand current practices and identify areas for improvement.

4.4 A Focus on Front Office Interactions

The front office operations at Fondazione Mondino represent an important step in the patient engagement strategy, as highlighted from the results of the previous sections of this chapter. It is among the first touchpoints between patients and the healthcare organization. This point of contact significantly influences patient perceptions and, more often than one could imagine, sets the tone for their entire healthcare journey at the organization. Given the complexity and stress associated with neurological conditions, it is essential that patients receive clear, compassionate, and efficient service from the very beginning. Therefore, the front office's role extends way beyond administrative tasks; it includes patient communication and often emotional support and some sort of guidance through the healthcare process.

Focus on the front office is of fundamental importance for several reasons: First, it serves as the entry point for patients, where first impressions are formed. The quality of interaction at this stage can affect patient satisfaction with the organization, but also adherence to treatment plans, and overall health outcomes. Second, the front office is where administrative processes such as appointment scheduling, check-ins, and initial consultations are managed, which can significantly impact patient wait times and their perception of organizational efficiency.

The "Innovation in Organization" project, led by Fondazione Mondino in collaboration with the Department of Economics and Management at the University of Pavia, underscored the necessity of optimizing front office operations to enhance resource efficiency, streamline processes, and improve the patient journey. This project involved a comprehensive analysis incorporating both qualitative and quantitative methodologies to identify the strengths and areas needing improvement within the front office services. Therefore, a deep investigation of the front office operations of Fondazione Mondino in 2023–2024 has revealed several challenges and opportunities for improvements.

At the heart of Fondazione Mondino's front office operations is a dedicated team of 13 staff members. This team is divided into two main groups: eight staff members manage direct patient interactions, while five support back-office functions. This division reflects the complex nature of front office operations, which encompass a wide range of tasks from appointment scheduling and check-ins to billing and admissions.

Our investigation revealed a nuanced approach to task management and staff development. Roles within the front office are clearly delineated, with some staff members already trained to handle all operations, while others are still in the training phase. Those in training typically focus on mastering a single type of operation (i.e., admissions or billing), indicating a structured, step-by-step approach to skill development. This approach allows for specialization while gradually building towards a multiskilled workforce.

However, this staffing structure also presents challenges. The relatively small team size compared to the volume and complexity of tasks can lead to increased pressure on staff, particularly during peak hours. Moreover, the absence of a dedicated reference figure apart from the Manager, who serves as the sole support for front office personnel, can sometimes lead to bottlenecks in problem-solving and decision-making processes.

Recognizing the need for a flexible and skilled workforce, Fondazione Mondino has implemented a cross-training program. This initiative aims to create a more versatile team capable of handling a wider range of front office tasks. A notable example of this commitment was a comprehensive training session held in August 2023, focused on familiarizing staff with a new management software system.

This push towards multifunctionality has the aim of improving operational flexibility. However, our investigation revealed a nuanced picture of its impact. Younger staff members generally embraced the opportunity to expand their skill sets, viewing it as a pathway to professional growth. In contrast, more tenured employees often found the transition challenging, expressing concerns about the rapid pace of change and the pressure to quickly master new systems and roles.

To facilitate the transition to multitasking, the institution has organized peer-to-peer training sessions. While this initiative demonstrates a commitment to skill development, some staff members expressed concerns about the tight timelines imposed for learning new competencies. This suggests a need for a more tailored, potentially longer-term approach to training that accounts for individual learning paces.

Another important aspect of the front office operations at Fondazione Mondino is about the technological advancements. A new management system was introduced in April 2023, which, after initial adaptation challenges, has been positively received by staff. They described it as intuitive and effective in improving work efficiency, particularly in areas such as appointment scheduling and patient data management.

However, the benefits of this technological advancement have not been yet fully realized and properly accepted across all staff members. Our observations revealed varying levels of proficiency with the new system, suggesting a need for ongoing, personalized training and support to ensure that technological improvements translate into consistently better patient experiences.

The challenge of balancing technological efficiency with human touch is perhaps most evident in the context of waiting times, a persistent pain point in patient satisfaction.

Our analysis of waiting time data over a 9-month period revealed fluctuations that often corresponded with periods of high patient volume or staff shortages. In fact, high wait times characterized by substantial delays were observed, especially during peak hours. For instance, patient influx peaks around 9:25 AM, creating bottlenecks. Patients with scheduled appointments often found themselves waiting beyond their appointment times, resulting in frustration and delays. Here follows Graph 4.1 showing the average waiting time per months, day of the week, and time slot, in the evaluated period of time (e.g., January–September 2023).

This issue was further emphasized by insufficient seating in the waiting area, forcing many patients to stand, and inadequately equipped children's areas, which added to the discomfort and dissatisfaction of waiting families. Therefore, we found that patients' perceptions of waiting times were not solely determined by the actual duration of the wait. Factors such as the clarity of communication about expected wait times, the comfort of the waiting area, and the perceived attentiveness of staff all played crucial roles in shaping patient satisfaction during these periods.

A key strength of Fondazione Mondino's front office operations is the proactive approach to quality improvement employed by the top management and, more specifically, by the front office manager himself. The practice of collecting daily feedback from the team and addressing operational issues allows for rapid identification and resolution of problems before they can significantly impact patient care. This continuous exchange of feedback between staff and the Manager highlights an open communication culture that aims to address issues promptly. This approach appears

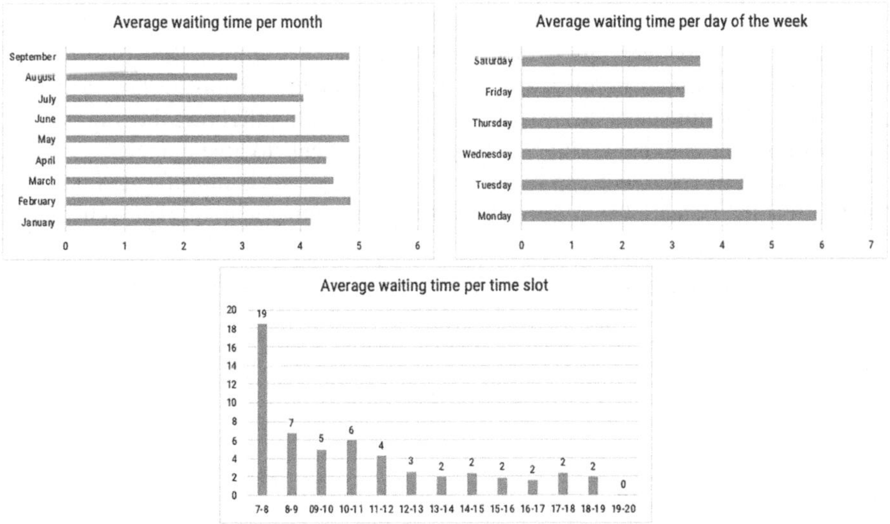

Graph 4.1 Average waiting time (in minutes). *Source*: own elaboration

to be a strength of the current management style, fostering a responsive and adaptive work environment.

However, our investigation also revealed opportunities to enhance this feedback system, particularly in capturing and integrating patient perspectives, but also in having to rely only on one person identified in the figure of the manager. While Fondazione Mondino does utilize customer satisfaction surveys, we found that these tools may not fully capture the nuances of front office interactions. Developing more targeted, real-time feedback mechanisms for this crucial touchpoint could provide valuable insights for continuous improvement.

4.4.1 Digital Transformation and Patient Engagement

In January 2024, Fondazione Mondino launched the Mondino Digital Service app, marking a significant step in their digital transformation journey. This initiative aimed at streamlining front office operations while also enhancing patient engagement. Our analysis of the app's usage data over its first 4 months reveals both promising trends and areas for improvement (see Graph 4.2), offering valuable insights into the challenges and opportunities of digital healthcare transformation.

The appointment booking feature has shown remarkable growth, with the number of appointments booked through the app increasing from just 16 in January to 133 in both March and April. This eightfold increase suggests a growing acceptance of digital tools among patients. However, it is important to note that these numbers, while encouraging, still represent a small fraction of the total appointments at Fondazione Mondino. This raises questions about how to further increase adoption rates and what barriers might be preventing wider use.

One potential strategy to boost app usage could be targeted patient education campaigns. Many patients, particularly older individuals or those less comfortable with technology, might be unaware of the app's benefits or unsure how to use it effectively. Providing clear, accessible instructions and highlighting the time-saving aspects of digital booking could encourage more patients to give it a try.

The impact of increased app usage on front office staff is multifaceted. On one hand, it has the potential to reduce the volume of routine appointment scheduling

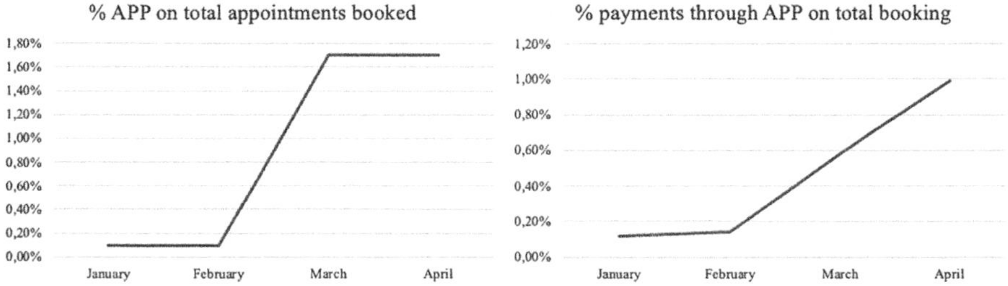

Graph 4.2 Mondino Digital Service app usage data. *Source*: Fondazione Mondino

calls, freeing up staff to focus on more complex patient needs. However, this shift also requires staff to develop new skills, such as guiding patients through digital processes. This evolution in staff responsibilities underscores the need for ongoing training and support to ensure that the front office team can effectively bridge the gap between digital and in-person patient care.

The app's payment feature shows a steady increase in adoption, with the percentage of payments made through the app rising from 0.12% in January to 0.99% in April. While this growth is positive, the overall numbers remain low, indicating significant room for improvement. Encouraging more patients to use digital payments could streamline financial processes and reduce administrative burdens. However, it is crucial to address potential concerns about security and ease of use that might be holding patients back from embracing this feature.

Perhaps the most intriguing data point comes from the check-in feature. After one check-in in January, usage dropped to zero for the following 3 months. This specific aspect warrants careful investigation. It could indicate technical issues, poor user experience design, or a lack of perceived value among patients. Understanding and addressing what causes patient to not use the app for check-ins, therefore not helping in reducing the waiting line at the front office of Fondazione Mondino, are crucial for the overall success of the app and its potential to enhance patient engagement.

The adoption rates across different app features highlight the complexity of digital transformation in healthcare. While patients seem ready to embrace some aspects of digital healthcare management, they may be hesitant about others. This uneven adoption presents both challenges and opportunities for patient engagement.

On the engagement front, the app has the potential to empower patients by giving them more control over their healthcare journey. The ability to book appointments and make payments at their convenience can reduce frustration and increase satisfaction. However, true engagement goes beyond mere transactions. The challenge lies in using the app as a platform for meaningful patient-provider communication and education.

For instance, the app could be expanded to include features such as personalized health information, appointment reminders with preparation instructions, or even secure messaging with healthcare providers. Such additions could transform the app from a simple administrative tool into a comprehensive patient engagement platform that not only covers the initial touchpoints of the patient's journey but could accompany the individual for the whole journey.

The impact on front office operations extends beyond just changing work processes. As more patients use the app for routine tasks, front office staff have the opportunity to provide more personalized, high-touch service to those who need it most. This could lead to improved patient satisfaction and outcomes, particularly for complex cases or patients requiring extra support.

However, realizing these benefits requires a careful approach. The risk of creating a "digital divide" among patients is real, with tech-savvy individuals potentially receiving faster, more efficient service, while others might face challenges navigating the new system. Fondazione Mondino must ensure that their digital transformation enhances rather than hinders accessibility and quality of care for all patients.

Looking ahead, the key to maximizing the app's potential lies in continuous improvement based on user feedback and data analysis. Regular surveys, user testing, and analysis of usage patterns can provide valuable insights for refining the various features as well as for improving user experience. Additionally, involving front office staff in the ongoing development of the app can ensure that it complements and enhances their work rather than complicating it.

Therefore, the introduction of the Mondino Digital Service app represents a promising step towards an improved patient engagement while streamlining front office operations. However, its value will be determined by how well Fondazione Mondino will be able to adapt and refine the app in response to patient needs and preferences. By viewing the app not as a standalone solution but as part of a broader patient engagement strategy, Fondazione Mondino will have the opportunity to create a more connected, efficient, and patient-centered healthcare experience.

4.4.2 Recommendations for Enhancing Patient Engagement in Front Office Operations

The case of Fondazione Mondino provides interesting insights on the challenges and opportunities for enhancing patient engagement during the first steps of the patient journey, namely, front office operations. On the bases of the main findings, we propose specific recommendations.

The introduction of the Mondino Digital Service app represents a significant step towards digital transformation. However, its uneven adoption across features suggests the need for a more integrated approach. As Prey et al. (2014) argue, successful patient engagement strategies often combine digital tools with personal interactions.

We recommend to develop better integration between the app and in-person front office services. For instance, patients who book appointments through the app could receive personalized guidance on arrival, potentially through a dedicated fast-track check-in process. This approach not only rewards app usage but also demonstrates the tangible benefits of digital engagement to other patients.

Then, the case highlighted the diverse reactions of staff to new technologies and multitasking requirements. As clear also from extant literature (e.g., Oladapo et al., 2023), healthcare staff play a crucial role in facilitating patient engagement. Here, we do not simply focus on healthcare professionals, like medical doctors or nurses, as one would expect. We underscore the importance of engaging also more administrative staff, like those at the front office, to support patient engagement along the whole patient journey. Therefore, we recommend implementing a more tailored, long-term approach to staff training that accounts for the different learning paces and prior experience of each individual whenever possible.

This could involve creating personalized learning paths for each staff member, combining online modules, peer-to-peer mentoring, and hands-on practice. Regular assessments could help identify areas where additional support is needed. Moreover, involving staff in the design and refinement of digital tools can increase its usage, ensuring that these tools improve their ability to engage with patients effectively.

Moreover, the analysis of waiting time at the front office reveals challenges that may significantly impact patient satisfaction. While digital solutions like the app can help, a more comprehensive approach might be actually needed. Drawing on the patient journey mapping (i.e., McCarthy et al., 2016), our recommendation on this matter involves implementing a proactive wait time management system. This could include, but it is not limited to, real-time updates on the wait times through either the app on the displays on-site, a virtual queue system that allows the individuals to leave the waiting area and return on time for their turn, or improving the comfort of the waiting area and providing engaging activities for both kids and adults.

By addressing both the actual and the perceived waiting time, Fondazione Mondino can enhance patient engagement from the moment they enter in the hospital facility.

A further recommendation regards the creation of a feedback ecosystem. As Hibbard and Greene (2013) argue, the more engaged patients also provide the best feedback for improving healthcare delivery. By treating patients as main informed actors or citizens/clients (Graffigna & Barello, 2017), the healthcare organization can indeed develop a patient journey based on their specific needs while increasing, at the same time, their engagement in the overall process.

To address this suggestion, a good approach could be implementing a multichannel feedback system that might include, but again is not limited to, real-time feedback options through the app after each interaction, short surveys at key points along the journey, focus groups, or even establishing a patient advisory board.

As previously mentioned, the different adoption rates of the various features of the app underlined the risk of creating a digital divide among patient groups. To be able to address this, healthcare organizations willing to advance in their digital journey must consider supporting patients' digital literacy by providing, for example, specific programs, in-person workshops, a dedicated helpline for digital support, or even partnerships with local communities or patient associations to reach the broader possible population sample. In order to be really effective, patient engagement's strategies should be used by the largest possible number of patients (Coulter, 2017).

Linked to the introduction of the Digital Service app, while the current version mainly focuses on appointment booking and payments, it opens up opportunities to transform it into a more comprehensive patient engagement platform. Drawing on the concept of the patient journey (e.g., Trebble et al., 2010), we suggest taking a step further in expanding the app's functionality to support patients throughout their entire experience at Fondazione Mondino.

The app could be enhanced to include personalized health information and educational resources tailored to individual patient needs. This would provide patients with knowledge about their conditions and treatments, all aspects that would instill a sense of control and involvement in their healthcare journey. Additionally, incorporating medication reminders or symptom-tracking tools would help patients manage their conditions more effectively, ensuring better adherence to treatment plans and enabling timely interventions when necessary. At the same time, having access to this information may also help healthcare professionals in better supporting patients and even provide data—in compliance with privacy and regulations—for enhancing and enriching research activities.

Another valuable addition would be to include virtual follow-up visits or consultations for suitable cases, offering patients the convenience of receiving care without the need to physically visit the hospital facility. This would be particularly beneficial, for example, for patients with mobility issues or those living in more remote or distant areas.

Finally, as already anticipated, the incredible amount of data generated through front office interactions and app usage presents an opportunity both for continuous improvement of the service and for research objectives—whenever in compliance with privacy regulations. We recommend implementing a data analytics strategy that combines operational metrics, patient feedback, and app usage data to identify trends and optimize engagement strategies. Data analysis could reveal patterns in patient behavior, preferences, and pain points that would in turn allow for specific and more targeted interventions.

References

Allena, M., Steiner, T. J., Sances, G., Carugno, B., Balsamo, F., Nappi, G., Andrée, C., & Tassorelli, C. (2015). Impact of headache disorders in Italy and the public-health and policy implications: A population-based study within the Eurolight project. *The Journal of Headache and Pain, 16*, 1–9.

Antonini, A., Moro, E., Godeiro, C., & Reichmann, H. (2018). Medical and surgical management of advanced Parkinson's disease. *Movement Disorders, 33*(6), 900–908.

Bandiera, P., Battaglia, M. A., Manacorda, T., & Zaratin, P. (2022). *BAROMETRO della Sclerosi Multipla e patologie correlate 2022*. Associazione Italiana Sclerosi Multipla APS. ISBN 9788871481579.

Barbanti, P. (2019). Le cefalee. Il parere dello specialista. *Rivista Società Italiana di Medicina Generale, 5*(26).

Bendtsen, L., Ashina, S., Moore, A., & Steiner, T. J. (2016). Muscles and their role in episodic tension-type headache: Implications for treatment. *European Journal of Pain, 20*(2), 166–175.

Bezzini, D., Battaglia, M. A., Ponzio, M., Manacorda, T., Zaratin, P., & Bandiera, P. (2020). Public health and multiple sclerosis in Italy. *European Journal of Public Health, 30*(Supplement_5), ckaa165-1105.

Bitner, M. J., Ostrom, A. L., & Morgan, F. N. (2008). Service blueprinting: A practical technique for service innovation. *California Management Review, 50*(3), 66–94.

Blaschke, S. J., Ellenberger, D., Flachenecker, P., Hellwig, K., Paul, F., Pöhlau, D., Kleinschnitz, C., Rommer, P. S., Rueger, M. A., Zettl, U. K., Stahmann, A., & Warnke, C. (2022). Time to diagnosis in multiple sclerosis: Epidemiological data from the German multiple sclerosis registry. *Multiple Sclerosis Journal, 28*(6), 865–871.

Bloem, B. R., Henderson, E. J., Dorsey, E. R., Okun, M. S., Okubadejo, N., Chan, P., Andrejack, J., Darweesh, S. K. L., & Munneke, M. (2020). Integrated and patient-centred management of Parkinson's disease: A network model for reshaping chronic neurological care. *The Lancet Neurology, 19*(7), 623–634.

Carman, K. L., Dardess, P., Maurer, M., Sofaer, S., Adams, K., Bechtel, C., & Sweeney, J. (2013). Patient and family engagement: A framework for understanding the elements and developing interventions and policies. *Health Affairs, 32*(2), 223–231.

Chaudhuri, K. R., Azulay, J. P., Odin, P., Lindvall, S., Domingos, J., Alobaidi, A., Kandukuri, P. L., Chaudhari, V. S., Parra, J. C., Yamazaki, T., Oddsdottir, J., Wright, J., & Martinez-Martin, P. (2024). Economic burden of Parkinson's disease: A multinational, real-world, cost-of-illness study. *Drugs-Real World Outcomes*, 1–11.

Coulter, A. (2017). Measuring what matters to patients. *BMJ, 356*, j816. https://doi.org/10.1136/bmj.j816. PMID: 28219884.

Crosier, A., & Handford, A. (2012). Customer journey mapping as an advocacy tool for disabled people: A case study. *Social Marketing Quarterly, 18*(1), 67–76.

Goadsby, P. J., Holland, P. R., Martins-Oliveira, M., Hoffmann, J., Schankin, C., & Akerman, S. (2017). Pathophysiology of migraine: A disorder of sensory processing. *Physiological Reviews*.

Graffigna, G., & Barello, S. (2017). The value of measuring patient engagement in healthcare: New frontiers for healthcare quality. In *Healthcare ethics and training: Concepts, methodologies, tools, and applications* (pp. 1268–1290). IGI Global.

Grafnna, G., & Barello, S. (2018). Patient health engagement (PHE) model in enhanced recovery after surgery (ERAS): Monitoring patients' engagement and psychological resilience in minimally invasive thoracic surgery. *Journal of Thoracic Disease, 10*(Suppl 4), S517.

Harley, A. (2015). *Personas make users memorable for product team members*. Nielsen Norman Group. https://www.nngroup.com/articles/persona/

Hauser, S. L., & Cree, B. A. (2020). Treatment of multiple sclerosis: A review. *The American Journal of Medicine, 133*(12), 1380–1390.

Hibbard, J. H., & Greene, J. (2013). What the evidence shows about patient activation: Better health outcomes and care experiences; fewer data on costs. *Health Affairs, 32*(2), 207–214.

Inojosa, H., Schriefer, D., & Ziemssen, T. (2020). Clinical outcome measures in multiple sclerosis: A review. *Autoimmunity Reviews, 19*(5), 102512.

Istituto Superiore di Sanità. (2018). Il contributo dei centri per i disturbi cognitivi e le demenze nella gestione integrata dei pazienti. Convegno 2018. https://www.epicentro.iss.it/parkinson/documentazione-italia

Lakin, L., Davis, B. E., Binns, C. C., Currie, K. M., & Rensel, M. R. (2021). Comprehensive approach to management of multiple sclerosis: Addressing invisible symptoms—A narrative review. *Neurology and Therapy, 10*, 75–98.

LeRouge, C., Ma, J., Sneha, S., & Tolle, K. (2013). User profiles and personas in the design and development of consumer health technologies. *International Journal of Medical Informatics, 82*(11), e251–e268.

Martelletti, P., Schwedt, T. J., Lanteri-Minet, M., Quintana, R., Carboni, V., Diener, H. C., de la Torre, E. R., Craven, A., Rasmussen, A. V., Evans, S., Laflamme, A. K., Fink, R., Walsh, D., Dumas, P., & Vo, P. (2018). My migraine voice survey: A global study of disease burden among individuals with migraine for whom preventive treatments have failed. *The Journal of Headache and Pain, 19*, 1–10.

McCarthy, S., O'Raghallaigh, P., Woodworth, S., Lim, Y. L., Kenny, L. C., & Adam, F. (2016). An integrated patient journey mapping tool for embedding quality in healthcare service reform. *Journal of Decision Systems, 25*(sup1), 354–368.

Oladapo, O. J., Afolabi, J. O. A., Olatoye, F. O., & Elufioye, O. A. (2023). Elevating patient care through human resources (HR) excellence in healthcare organizations. *World Journal of Advanced Research and Reviews, 20*(3), 345–362.

Osservatorio Malattie Rare (2023). Parkinson: 300 mila italiani colpiti dalla patologia. Retrieved on June 2024, and available at: https://www.osservatoriomalattierare.it/malattia-di-parkinson/20192-parkinson-300mila-gli-italianicolpiti-dalla-patologia.

Paz-Zulueta, M., Parás-Bravo, P., Cantarero-Prieto, D., Blázquez-Fernández, C., & Oterino-Durán, A. (2020). A literature review of cost-of-illness studies on the economic burden of multiple sclerosis. *Multiple Sclerosis and Related Disorders, 43*, 102162.

Poewe, W., Seppi, K., Tanner, C. M., Halliday, G. M., Brundin, P., Volkmann, J., Schrag, A.-E., & Lang, A. E. (2017). Parkinson disease. *Nature Reviews Disease Primers, 3*(1), 1–21.

Prey, J. E., Woollen, J., Wilcox, L., Sackeim, A. D., Hripcsak, G., Bakken, S., Restaino, S., Feiner, S., & Vawdrey, D. K. (2014). Patient engagement in the inpatient setting: A systematic review. *Journal of the American Medical Informatics Association, 21*(4), 742–750.

Riccò, M., Vezzosi, L., Balzarini, F., Gualerzi, G., Ranzieri, S., Signorelli, C., Colucci, M. E., & Bragazzi, N. L. (2020). Prevalence of Parkinson disease in Italy: A systematic review and meta-analysis. *Acta Bio Medica: Atenei Parmensis, 91*(3), e2020088.

Sacco, S., Braschinsky, M., Ducros, A., Lampl, C., Little, P., Van Den Brink, A. M., Pozo-Rosich, P., Reuter, U., de la Torre, E. R., Sanchez Del Rio, M., Sinclair, A. J., Katsara, Z., & Martelletti, P. (2020). European headache federation consensus on the definition of resistant and refractory migraine: Developed with the endorsement of the European Migraine & Headache Alliance (EMHA). *The Journal of Headache and Pain, 21*, 1–12.

Sarchielli, P., Granella, F., Prudenzano, M. P., Pini, L. A., Guidetti, V., Bono, G., Pinessi, L., Alessandri, M., Antonaci, F., Fanciullacci, M., Ferrari, A., Guazelli, M., Nappi, G., Sances, G., Sandrini, G., Savi, L., Tassorelli, C., & Zanchin, G. (2012). Italian guidelines for primary headaches: 2012 revised version. *The Journal of Headache and Pain, 13*, 31–70.

Schapira, A. H., Chaudhuri, K. R., & Jenner, P. (2017). Non-motor features of Parkinson disease. *Nature Reviews Neuroscience, 18*(7), 435–450.

Steiner, T. J., Jensen, R., Katsarava, Z., Linde, M., MacGregor, E. A., Osipova, V., Paemeleire, K., Olesen, J., Peters, M., & Martelletti, P. (2019). Aids to management of headache disorders in primary care on behalf of the European headache federation and lifting the burden: The global campaign against headache. *The Journal of Headache and Pain, 20*, 1–52.

Stovner, L. J., Nichols, E., Steiner, T. J., Abd-Allah, F., Abdelalim, A., Al-Raddadi, R. M., et al. (2018). Global, regional, and national burden of migraine and tension-type headache, 1990–2016: A systematic analysis for the global burden of disease study 2016. *The Lancet Neurology, 17*(11), 954–976.

Tassorelli, C., Diener, H. C., Silberstein, S. D., Dodick, D. W., Goadsby, P. J., Jensen, R. H., Magis, D., Pozo-Rosich, P., Yuan, H., Martinelli, D., van den Hoek, T., Deen, M., Ashina, M., & Terwindt, G. M. (2021). Guidelines of the international headache society for clinical trials with neuromodulation devices for the treatment of migraine. *Cephalalgia, 41*(11–12), 1135–1151.

Trebble, T. M., Hansi, N., Hydes, T., Smith, M. A., & Baker, M. (2010). Process mapping the patient journey: An introduction. *BMJ, 341*.

Van Hijfte, L., Cambron, M., Capron, B., Dachy, B., Decoo, D., Dive, D., Dubois, B., El Sankari, S., London, F., Perrotta, G., Papescu, V., Van Pesch, V., Van Wijmeersch, B., Willekens, B., & Laureys, G. (2024). Multiple sclerosis multidisciplinary care: A National Survey and lessons for the global community. *Multiple Sclerosis and Related Disorders, 85*, 105540.

Vanacore, N., & Morgante, L. (2001). *Epidemiologia dei parkinsonismi. La malattia di Parkinson ei disturbi del movimento* (pp. 1–20). CIC Edizioni Internazionali.

Chapter 5
Organization and Patient Engagement at Front Office: A Proposed Framework

Abstract The Patient Engagement at Front Office (PEFO) framework addresses an important yet underexplored touchpoint in patient-centered care: the front office. Built on insights from a systematic literature review and a case study at Fondazione Mondino IRCCS, PEFO highlights five interconnected components: digital integration, staff empowerment, environment optimization, information clarity, and feedback loops. This structured approach improves early-stage engagement, shaping patient perceptions and enhancing organizational efficiency. By integrating tailored digital tools, empowering staff, and fostering clear communication, PEFO offers actionable strategies to optimize patient experience from the outset.While further validation across diverse healthcare context is needed. PEFO provides a robust foundation for prioritizing patient engagement and streamlining operational processes.

5.1 Introduction

The healthcare landscape is rapidly evolving, and patient engagement has emerged as a critical factor in delivering high-quality, patient-centered care. Extant studies have shown that engaged patients are more likely to adhere to treatment plans, experience better health outcomes, and report higher satisfaction with their care (Moody-Williams, 2020; Pierz et al., 2024; Porter, 2022). However, despite the growing recognition of the importance of patient engagement, many healthcare organizations struggle to implement effective strategies, particularly in the early stages of the patient journey.

This chapter proposed an approach to enhancing patient engagement and organizational efficiency, focusing on one of the most crucial yet often overlooked and understudy touchpoints: the front office. Drawing from our comprehensive analysis of patient engagement strategies and their impact on healthcare organizations' efficiency, we propose the Patient Engagement at Front Office (PEFO) framework.

F. Sanguineti, *The Organizational Impact of Patient Engagement*, SpringerBriefs in Business, https://doi.org/10.1007/978-3-031-77964-0_5

Thus, this framework aims to address the critical first touchpoint in the patient journey, recognizing its crucial role in shaping patient perceptions and subsequent engagement throughout the care process The framework is grounded in insights derived from a systematic literature review and a case study analysis of Fondazione Mondino, a leading healthcare institution in Italy.

Therefore, it aims to address one of the gaps identified in our systematic literature review, namely, the need for tailored strategies to enhance patient engagement in the early stages of the patient journey, necessity that has been further highlighted by the findings from our case study analysis.

The PEFO framework consists of five core components: digital integration, staff empowerment, environment optimization, information clarity, and feedback loop. Each of these elements is designed to address specific aspects of front office engagement while collectively providing a structured approach to enhancing the patient experience since the beginning of their interaction with the healthcare organization.

To illustrate the challenges and potential impact of the PEFO framework, consider the story of Maria, a 65-year-old patient visiting a healthcare facility for the first time. As she enters the front office, she is greeted by a confusing array of signage, long wait times, and staff who seem too busy to answer her questions. This experience leaves Maria feeling frustrated, setting a negative tone for her entire healthcare journey. Now, imagine if the same facility had implemented the PEFO framework. Maria would be greeted by a welcoming environment, user-friendly digital tools for check-in and information access, and empowered staff trained to provide clear, personalized guidance. This positive front office experience would lay the foundation for Maria's continued engagement throughout her care journey.

The PEFO framework represents a structured approach to patient engagement, offering healthcare organizations a tool to investigate and identify strategies to drive organization-level improvements in patient engagement.

In the following sections, we will delve into the development of the PEFO framework, explore its five core components, and provide practical guidelines for its implementation. We will also discuss the potential impact and contributions of this framework to the field of healthcare management, as well as its limitations and future research directions.

5.1.1 Framework Development

The development of the Patient Engagement at Front Office (PEFO) framework is grounded on the insights derived from both the literature analysis and the study on patient journeys at Fondazione Mondino.

Among the avenues for future research highlighted in the first chapter of this book and based on the findings of the systematic literature review, investigating patient engagement in the early stages of the patient journey emerges as a key point.

This got validated in the results of our case study analysis. The willingness—translated into strategic lines—of Fondazione Mondino to become patient-centered and the potential opportunities recognized by the top management to revise front office operations are clear indicators. Moreover, having the chance to put into practice strategies at the organization level that can help increase the overall patient engagement is of outmost importance. Therefore, we identified the front office as a crucial touchpoint that significantly influences patient perceptions and future engagement. This insight highlighted the need for a targeted framework to enhance patient engagement at this initial stage of the healthcare journey.

A thorough examination of current front office operations at Fondazione Mondino revealed both best practices and areas for improvement. We analyzed factors such as organizational structures, team management, technological tools, and patient feedback mechanisms to understand the intricacies of front office engagement.

By comparing and contrasting the findings from both the general and more specific patient journeys and the overall front office analysis, we identified common themes that cut across the various departments. These themes included the importance of digital integration, staff empowerment, environment improvement, information clarity, and continuous feedback loops. Thus, building upon these main themes, we defined five core components, each designed to address a specific aspect of front office engagement while collectively providing a potential approach to enhancing the patient experience. It has to be noted that these five elements are strongly interconnected. For instance, the effectiveness of digital tools (*digital integration*) is closely tied to the ability of staff to guide patients in their use (*staff empowerment*), while the clarity of information provided (*information clarity*) can influence the overall patient experience in the front office environment (*environment optimization*).

To stress on the practical applicability of the PEFO framework, we developed a set of implementation guidelines based on experiences, challenges, and opportunities derived from the case study analysis. These guidelines provide a roadmap for healthcare organizations to assess their current front office engagement levels, prioritize areas for improvement, develop action plans, and evaluate and refine their strategies.

5.1.2 The Patient Engagement Front Office (PEFO) Framework

The PEFO framework is, therefore, a comprehensive approach that could help in enhancing patient engagement at the beginning of the patient journey. This framework consists of five main elements (see Fig. 5.1) that are strongly interconnected and that should all be considered when evaluating potential strategies to implement at the front office stage of the process.

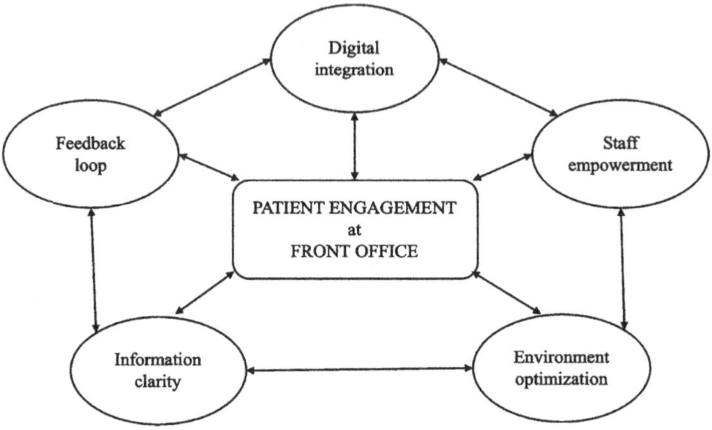

Fig. 5.1 Proposed framework for Patient Engagement at Front Office (PEFO). *Source:* own elaboration

The first component of the PEFO framework is *digital integration*. This element recognizes the increasingly digital nature of social interactions. It reflects the importance of leveraging technology to enhance the patient experience from the beginning of their journey. It involves implementing user-friendly digital tools for essential front office functions such as appointment scheduling, check-ins, and information access. These digital solutions should be designed in a way that it could be easily integrated with the organization's electronic health record system, not only ensuring a smooth flow of information but also reducing administrative burden.

By offering patients the convenience of digital interactions, healthcare organizations can not only improve efficiency but also cater to the preferences of tech-savvy patients while providing support for those less comfortable with technology.

Complementing the digital aspect, *staff empowerment* highlights the human core of the PEFO framework. This component emphasizes the critical role of front office staff in shaping patient perceptions and experiences. It calls for comprehensive training programs that go beyond basic administrative skills to encompass advanced communication techniques, empathy development, and cultural competence. By investing in staff development, healthcare organizations can create a front office team capable of handling diverse patient needs with empathy and professionalism. This empowerment extends to giving staff the authority to make decisions that can immediately improve patient experiences, fostering a sense of ownership and dedication to patient engagement. The healthcare organization should set roles and define boundaries for authority delegation to the front office staff and at the same time identify with the Head of each department what is needed at this specific point of contact with their patients in order to plan in advance how to better engage patients at the very beginning. This should make departments feel more active in this step as well and the organization more responsive to patients' and departments' needs.

The third component, *environment optimization*, incorporates both physical and digital spaces where initial patient interactions occur. This element emphasizes creating welcoming, efficient, and stress-reducing environments. In the physical realm, this might involve thoughtful layout design, comfortable seating arrangements, and clear signage. In the digital space, it translates to intuitive designs and user-friendly interfaces for patient portals. This might also include specific check-in priority lines or actual maps to help in the physical movement from one spot to the other—for example, where to go for the visit, in which office, or for specific exams. The goal should be to create an atmosphere that puts patients at comfort from the moment they enter the healthcare facility or access its digital platforms, setting a positive tone for their entire journey.

The third element, identified in *information clarity*, focuses on the importance of offering clear, accessible, and personalized information. This component addresses the often-overwhelming nature of healthcare information by advocating for tailored communication strategies. It involves developing pre-visit communications that prepare patients for their appointments, creating easily understandable educational materials, and training staff to convey complex medical information in easy and understandable-to-everyone language. By making sure that patients have access to the information they need in a format they can understand, healthcare organizations can empower patients to take a more active role in their care from the very beginning.

The final component, *feedback loop*, completes the framework by establishing a system for continuous improvement. This element involves not just collecting patient feedback regarding their front office experiences but also analyzing this data and, more importantly, acting upon it. By creating channels for patients to share their experiences and perspectives, healthcare organizations can gain valuable insights into the effectiveness of their engagement strategies. This ongoing feedback mechanism allows for rapid identification of areas for improvement and helps in tailoring services to meet evolving patient needs and expectations.

Together, these five components have an impact on engaging the patient in their own journeys, since the very beginning. This can affect not only the outcome of the care—given the increase participation and the shared decision-making—but also the overall satisfaction of patients which, in turn, could lead to higher organizational efficiency on various levels. A part from potentially increasing the number of patients, given the positive word of mouth, the PEFO framework could contribute in streamlining front office processes through digital integration and staff empowerment. Healthcare organizations can potentially reduce the time and resources spent on administrative tasks. Moreover, among other aspects, by optimizing the front office environment and providing clearer information, healthcare organizations could improve patient flow.

Therefore, the PEFO framework represents a step forward in operationalizing patient engagement principles at the first point of contact in healthcare organizations. By focusing on this often under-explored aspect of the patient journey, the framework offers a practical tool for healthcare providers to enhance patient satisfaction, improve operational efficiency, and ultimately contribute to better health outcomes. Its flexibility allows for adaptation across various healthcare settings, making it a valuable resource for organizations seeking to prioritize patient-centered care from the very first interaction.

Implementation Guidelines

The successful implementation of the Patient Engagement Front Office (PEFO) Framework requires a structured approach that should be tailored to the unique context of each healthcare organization. The following guidelines provide a roadmap, summarized in Fig. 5.2, for healthcare organizations seeking to enhance patient engagement starting at the front office level.

The organization that wants to adopt patient engagement strategies at the front office should start by identifying a team that will be responsible for the whole process. Among the individuals involved, there should be representatives from various areas, including top management team and healthcare providers, but also, even if only for some dedicated steps, representatives of the front office staff. The team will be equipped to drive changes and oversee implementation progresses.

The first task is to assess the current situation (AS-IS) by conducting a thorough evaluation of the organization's existing front office operations and patient engagement levels. This assessment involves mapping current front office processes and technologies; analyzing patient feedback and satisfaction data; evaluating staff roles, responsibilities, and training needs; and assessing the physical and digital front office environments. To facilitate this assessment, visual elements can be incorporated into the PEFO framework graphic, such as checkboxes or color-coded indicators, helping stakeholders quickly identify areas of strength and improvement opportunities.

Based on the assessment findings, the implementation team should define the desired state (TO-BE) by setting clear goals and objectives for enhancing patient engagement and front office efficiency. These goals should align with the organization's overall mission and strategic priorities. Visualizing these goals within the PEFO framework, using elements such as target KPIs, timelines, or benchmarks, can help in better visualizing the expected outcomes.

Once the specifics for the "TO-BE" state are defined, the implementation team should prioritize the main areas for improvement based on the organization's specific needs and available resources. This step involves identifying the most pressing issues and opportunities that will have the greatest impact on patient engagement and front office efficiency. These priorities could also be, and it is even suggested,

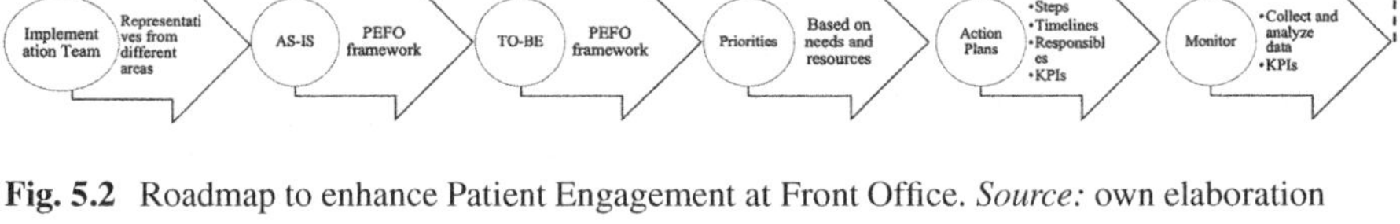

Fig. 5.2 Roadmap to enhance Patient Engagement at Front Office. *Source:* own elaboration

small first steps to the implementation of a bigger plan. For example, introducing an app for booking and check-ins to use as the starting base for a platform that will then be integrated based on users' feedback could be the first priority, rather than implementing a whole platform that already includes it all, which might entail a way bigger commitment in terms of costs as well as human resources' adaptation to changes. The team should consider factors such as the feasibility of implementation, potential benefits, and alignment with organizational goals when determining priorities.

For each prioritized component, the implementation team should develop a detailed action plan outlining specific steps, timelines, and responsible parties. These action plans should include clear objectives and deliverables, resource requirements (e.g., technology investments, training programs), key performance indicators (KPIs) to track progress and success, and risk assessment and mitigation strategies. Example of KPIs could include the percentage of appointments booked through digital channels, staff training completion rates, and patient satisfaction scores related to front office experiences.

As the action plans are implemented, the team should regularly collect and analyze data on the previously defined KPIs. Sharing progress updates with stakeholders and celebrating successes along the way helps with the engagement. On the hand, monitoring the progresses might also highlight potential misalignment, thus offering the opportunity to address potential challenges as they come and adapt the plan accordingly. The team should conduct periodic reviews to identify areas for improvement and make data-driven adjustments to the strategies, whenever necessary.

It is important to note that implementing the PEFO framework is an ongoing process. Therefore, it should not be seen as one-time event. After the monitoring phase, the implementation team should go back to the "AS-IS" step to reassess the current situation and identify new opportunities for improvement. As patient needs evolve and new technologies emerge, the implementation team should continuously reevaluate the front office engagement strategies and adapt them to maintain relevance and effectiveness or enlarge its scope including features that might help also in future steps of the patient journey. Encouraging a culture of continuous improvement, where staff at all levels are empowered to suggest ideas and drive positive change, is important for long-term success of patient engagement strategies and organizational efficiency.

Impact and Contributions

The Patient Engagement at Front Office framework addresses a gap identified in our systematic literature review, which highlights the need for tailored strategies to enhance patient engagement in the early stages of the patient journey. This necessity has been further validated by the findings from the case study analysis of Fondazione Mondino. Indeed, it was identified as a crucial starting point for implementing effective patient engagement practices, with Fondazione Mondino already starting to put it into practice. By targeting the front office as a key touchpoint, the PEFO framework has the potential to impact patient experiences, organizational efficiency, patient care efficiency, revenue growth, cost management, and financial stability, offering contributions to both theory and practice in healthcare management.

In terms of theoretical contribution, the PEFO framework enriches the existing body of knowledge by focusing on patient engagement strategies within front office operations. Here, patient engagement strategies are considered at the organization level rather than on specific departments level. Studies have shown that it is important to engage patients throughout their whole journey (Pierz et al., 2024; Porter, 2022) and that involving them in the decision-making process can increase patient adherence, thus leading to better health outcomes, while also potentially reducing associated costs (Marzban et al., 2022). By focusing on the front office, the PEFO framework highlights the importance of improving the engagement at early-stage patient interactions while also underlining tactics and strategies that should be put in place at the organizational level to support the overall patient engagement.

From a practical point of view, the PEFO framework offers healthcare organizations an actionable approach to enhancing patient engagement and efficiency at the front office level. The five key components of the framework—digital integration, staff empowerment, environment optimization, information clarity, and feedback loop—provide a clear structure for healthcare managers to assess their current front office operations, identify areas for improvement, and implement targeted strategies. By offering a structured approach to front office engagement, the PEFO framework enables healthcare organizations to operationalize patient-centered care principles and drive tangible improvements in patient experiences that could be reflected on more positive organizational outcomes.

Implementing the PEFO framework can lead to improved patient care efficiency by reducing wait times, streamlining check-in processes, and providing patients with the information they need to actively participate in their care. By optimizing the front office environment and leveraging digital tools, healthcare organizations can create a more seamless and efficient patient experience, ultimately contributing to better health outcomes.

Moreover, the PEFO framework can indirectly contribute to revenue growth by enhancing patient satisfaction and loyalty, which may lead to increased patient retention and referrals. By streamlining front office processes and reducing administrative burden through digital integration and staff empowerment, healthcare organizations can potentially lower operational costs and reallocate resources to other areas of patient care.

While the direct impact of the PEFO framework on financial stability may be limited, it can contribute to the overall financial health of healthcare organizations by improving operational efficiency and patient satisfaction. By creating a more engaging and efficient front office experience, healthcare organizations can potentially reduce patient churn, increase market share, and enhance their reputation, all of which can contribute to long-term financial stability.

The proposed framework's potential to drive improvements in various aspects of healthcare organizations' operations, such as reducing administrative burden and increasing patient adherence and retention, further underscores its practical significance. By offering a targeted approach to front office engagement, the framework enables healthcare organizations to find ways to optimize resource allocation, streamline processes, and ultimately improve the quality and efficiency of care delivery. These practical implications highlight the framework's potential to generate tangible benefits for healthcare organizations, their staff, and the patients they serve.

While the case study is specific to Fondazione Mondino, the insights gained from this institution and integrated with an in-depth literature review on the topic that resulted in the PEFO framework can be useful for other healthcare organizations, especially in the Italian context. The framework's emphasis on adapting strategies for different organizations at different points in time and its focus on the front office as a fundamental touchpoint for engagement may be particularly beneficial for other specialized hospitals and research centers, like IRCCS. By adapting and implementing the PEFO framework to their specific contexts, these organizations can support in enhancing patient engagement while improving operational efficiency. The results will also contribute to better health outcomes for the populations they serve.

Limitations and Future Steps

While the PEFO framework offers an approach to enhancing patient engagement and organizational efficiency in healthcare settings, it is essential to acknowledge its limitations and identify potential future steps that will enrich it.

One of the primary limitations of the PEFO framework is the scarcity of empirical evidence supporting its effectiveness in diverse healthcare contexts. Although the framework draws upon existing literature and the case study of Fondazione Mondino, further research is needed to validate its applicability and generalizability across different healthcare systems. Future studies should focus on implementing the framework in various settings and evaluating its impact on patient engagement, organizational efficiency, and health outcomes using rigorous methodological approaches.

Another limitation is the potential challenge of integrating it into existing healthcare organizational structures and processes. Implementing the framework may require significant changes in organizational culture, staff training, and resource allocation. Healthcare organizations may struggle to allocate sufficient resources to support the implementation of the framework. Future research should explore the barriers and facilitators to implementing PEFO and develop strategies to overcome these challenges.

Furthermore, the PEFO framework primarily focuses on the front office as a key touchpoint for patient engagement. While this focus is essential, it may not fully capture the complexity of the patient journey and the multiple factors that influence patient engagement beyond the front office. Future research should examine how it can be integrated with other patient engagement strategies across the entire continuum of care, from prevention to follow-up.

Finally, the long-term sustainability and cost-effectiveness of implementing PEFO remain to be determined. While the framework has the potential to improve organizational structure, the initial investment in staff training, technology, and process redesign may be substantial. Future research should conduct cost-benefit analyses to assess the long-term financial viability of implementing the PEFO framework and explore strategies to ensure its sustainability over time.

5.2 Concluding Remarks

The proposed framework is a step forward in operationalizing patient engagement principles at one of the first points of contacts in healthcare organizations. Built upon the insights from a systematic literature review and the case study of Fondazione Mondino, the PEFO framework provides a structured approach to enhancing patient engagement with strategies at the organizational level. While the framework's effectiveness in diverse healthcare contexts requires further validation, it provides a valuable starting point for healthcare organizations seeking to prioritize patient-centered care and drive improvements in care delivery. As the healthcare landscape continues to evolve, the strategies and recommendations presented in this book can guide healthcare managers, researchers, and practitioners in their efforts to create a more responsive, efficient, and patient-centric healthcare system.

References

Marzban, S., Najafi, M., Agolli, A., & Ashrafi, E. (2022). Impact of patient engagement on healthcare quality: A scoping review. *Journal of Patient Experience, 9*, 23743735221125439.

Moody-Williams, J. (2020). *A journey towards patient-centered healthcare quality*. Springer International Publishing.

Pierz, K. A., Locantore, N., McCreary, G., Calvey, R. J., Hackney, N., Doshi, P., Linnell, J., Sundaramoorthy, A., Reed, C. R., & Yates, J. (2024). Investigation of the impact of Wellinks on the quality of life and clinical outcomes in patients with chronic obstructive pulmonary disease: Interventional research study. *JMIR Formative Research, 8*, e47555.

Porter, L. D. (2022). The importance of patient engagement to improve healthcare research and safety. *Global Journal on Quality and Safety in Healthcare, 5*(2), 27–30.

The manufacturer's authorised representative in the EU is Springer Nature Customer Service Centre GmbH, Europaplatz 3, 69115 Heidelberg, Germany. If you have any concerns regarding our products, please contact ProductSafety@springernature.com

Printed and bound by CPI Group (UK) Ltd, Croydon, CR0 4YY
01/10/2026
02225839-0006